They Knew Their God

Volume 3

They Knew Their God

Volume 3

E. F. & L. Harvey

UNITED STATES ADDRESS
Harvey Christian Publishers, Inc.
449 Hackett Pike, Richmond, KY 40475
Tel./Fax (423) 768-2297
E-mail: books@harveycp.com
www.harveycp.com

ISBN 978-1-932774-11-5

Printed by
Lightning Source Inc.
La Vergne, TN 37086

Contents

Authors' Preface

We have continued to fullfil what we believe to have been God's purpose in walking about spiritual Zion, marking her bulwarks, her palaces, and her towers, and then prayerfully and after much biographical research, relating our interesting discoveries to a coming generation. The Church of today, for the most part, has drifted so far from Biblical Christianity that many of the later generations do not know of men and women of the past who knew their God in such an intimate way that they performed His counsel, fulfilled His purposes, and left us a legacy of infinite worth.

The particular characters in Books Three and Four have been chosen because in them there was a Divine Purpose manifest, and a Divine influence felt. They heard a voice and followed; they wrestled with their sinful natures and saw in Redemption a cure for their sin; they grappled with almost insurmountable difficulties but overcame. There is evidence that they possessed within themselves an indwelling Spirit Who moved them with compassion for the unlovable and supplied them with resources from a Heavenly base.

The Holy Spirit, a present-day Resident, moved upon their hearts to do God's will. Was there a heathen tribe unevangelized? The Lord of Harvest knew where to find His prepared vessel to fill that need! Was it a tribe who needed the Word of God in their own language? He knew whom to call as a translator! Was it a downtrodden race overrun by selfish overlords? He had His deliverer. Had Churchmen tried to denude the Bible of its glorious inspiration? He knew men, mighty in the Scripture, to restore it to its pristine glory! Was it to be an intercessor? He could whisper His call to travail and place His groanings within those willing for the inconvenience!

The Acts of the Apostles did not end two thousand years ago, but His disciples have all down through the centuries quietly moved out into ripened harvest fields. God has never lacked His Peters to go to the household of a Cornelius; His Pauls ready for Gentile peoples; His Stephens prepared for one brief sermon in which a Saul of Tarsus is pricked with the goads of the Almighty; His Philips who are so consecrated they can leave a revival and go desert way to meet one enquiring, Ethiopian Eunuch. He still has His unknown Ananiases ready to face death in order to go behind shut doors where a praying figure needs illumination.

The religious world, so busy and noisy with its man-planned campaigns and philanthropies, is not aware of that silent host moving still by a pillar of fire, guided still by the Lord of Hosts to conquests unrecognized because so seemingly small and silent. Having no spiritual eyes to detect His pathway on the sea, or spiritual ears to hear His still, small voice in quiet command, and no quickened spirit to know the Caanans still to be possessed, such worldlings cannot possibly understand such servants of God. Because unrecognized, these saints of God go on unimpeded by carnal Christians, completing their heaven-sent task. God gifted them with thorns in the flesh and with cracks in their earthen vessels in order to protect them. He has permitted their lives, in many cases, to be preserved for us in biographies, diaries, and magazines. How we pray that these readings may stimulate Christians of our day to expect a close relationship with their God so that they too might fulfil, in our needy time, the will of the Father.

I am grateful for the faithful labors of Edward Cook, Trudy Tait, and Joan Henry in making this publication possible. I am also deeply indebted to my dear husband for his former work on some of these sketches, and for the privilege of continuing his ministry so that he, being dead, yet speaketh.

Lillian G. Harvey, Hampton, Tennessee
July, 1988

Publishers' Foreword

They Knew Their God, Volume Three was first published in 1988, and, having been reproduced from the original several times, we thought it time to reset the book completely.

In our more recent publications, we cite the page and book from which each quotation has been taken. In the first edition of this book, this was not done, so we have gone to considerable pains to discover the sources for these quotations. When possible, we have listed these in the back under "Notes to Sources."

My husband and I now publish this new edition of *They Knew Their God, Volume Three* with thankfulness for the blessing it has been to so many over the years, and with the prayer that it may continue to challenge all of us to "Know our God" in a richer, fuller, and more abandoned way.

Trudy and Barry Tait, Hampton, Tennessee
March, 2007

My goal is God Himself, not joy, nor peace,
   Nor even blessing, by Himself my God.
'Tis His to lead me there⁻ not mine, but His⁻
   At any cost, dear Lord, by any road.

So faith bounds forward to its goal in God,
   And love can trust her Lord to lead her there;
Upheld by Him, my soul is following hard
   Till God hath full fulfilled my deepest prayer.

No matter if the way be sometimes dark,
   No matter though the cost be oft-times great,
He knoweth how I best shall reach the mark,
   The way that leads to Him must needs be strait.

One thing I know, I cannot say Him nay;
   One thing I do, I press towards my Lord;
My God my glory here, from day to day,
   And in the glory there my great Reward.

                    ⁻Frederick Brook.

Marquis De Renty

THE NOBLEMAN WHO STEPPED DOWN

A young science student of seventeen on his way home from the University of Paris would often stop to browse among the second-hand books before returning to his lodgings. One day the bookseller pressed him to take the book *Imitation of Christ* by Thomas à Kempis. At first the young man was not in the least interested, but after continued pressure he finally yielded. The perusal of a book has very definitely changed the life direction of more than one famous person, and it was so in this case, for the reading of this volume had such a profound effect upon the student that he directed his life into completely different channels from that time on.

The Marquis de Renty, for the young science student was none other than he, was born in 1611 in the Château Beny in Normandy, France. His well-to-do parents had high ambitions for their son, but after perusing the *Imitation of Christ*, the young nobleman came to despise the demands which society placed upon such as he.

One day, when driving with his mother through Paris, De Renty managed to make his escape. In a letter written to his father from the safe retreat of a monastery, he wrote that the maxims which govern the Christian vary so from the habits of the world that he did not feel strong enough to withstand the pressures that would be placed upon him were he to remain in his former position. It was evident from the letter that he was trying to run away from the opposition which would cause him to become "everyone's song." He knew only too well that to follow Christ would bring the inevitable cross, and so he sought shelter under the umbrella of a religious community.

His father was unyielding and finally, after a thorough search, found him at Amboise and took him back to his home in Beny. As time went by, the complete transformation in young De Renty's life became evident and gained him general respect.

When twenty-two, he married a singularly good woman and began to take up the duties which were associated with a Frenchman of means. He was expected to spend some time in the army, which he did, and by his prayerful life influenced others for good. He was likewise expected to attend the royal court, but instead, he disappointed such expectations, choosing rather to faithfully perform what he considered to be his duty in managing a large estate.

It was now that he formed habits of a devout life, spending two or three hours in prayer, in heat or in cold. From his own writings we get a glimpse of his rigorous manner of life:

> I generally rise at five o'clock (after having spent a part of the night in prayer). As soon as I wake I sink myself into my ground of nothingness before the divine Majesty. After rising I fall on my knees and adore the benefit of the Incarnation which gives us access to God. After dressing (on which I do not spend much time) I go into my chapel and kneel down to worship God. I hold myself before Him as an empty vessel and think of myself as low and needy. I keep my heart in this disposition, then take refuge in God's Holy Son and His Spirit, desiring to please Him in all things. Then I read in the New Testament, and, after a brief meditation, go to my work.
>
> Before midday dinner there is another period of prayer. During the meal a helpful book is read. Afterward an hour is spent talking with people who wish to see me. Then I go out where God leads me; if there is nothing special I often enter a church and pray there; every evening an hour is again given

to prayer. During supper a portion from the lives of saints and martyrs is read; after supper I have a talk with my children. At nine o'clock I have prayers with them and the domestic staff; then all leave me, and I remain in prayer till ten o'clock.[1]

It might indeed be said of De Renty as it was said of Enoch, "He walked with God."

> I walk with God!
> Earth's rising din of battle may surround me,
> Man's many dread inventions may astound me;
> I fear not, for His arm is thrown around me;
> I walk with God.
>
> I walk with God;
> Though clouds may threaten in the sky above me,
> Though storms of fear and hate sweep down to move me,
> There is no fear in love⁻ and He doth love me;
> I walk with God.
>
> I walk with God,
> Adversity or guile may overtake me,
> And brethren⁻ true or false⁻ may oft mistake me;
> I need not fear, for He will not forsake me,
> I walk with God.
>
> I walk with God,
> I have no strength to walk without His power,
> But when the clock of Heaven peals out the hour,
> My hand in His, past Zion's shining tower
> I'll walk with God.
>
> *⁻ William Montgomery.*

As the young nobleman grew in grace, he became more simple in his habits; reading the life of Christ doubtless caused him to dispense with superfluities. Once, when he was expected at a social function, he did not arrive, and was discovered to be eating a meal with the prisoners in a nearby jail. Unknown to others, he would light the fires in the grates of the poor, take food to the hungry and listen to their troubles, making himself available to those in need. He would frequently visit the place where the destitute congregated, taking them to his own home where he and his children would feed and serve them with their own hands.

As De Renty grew still more familiar with the life of Christ, he progressed in the practice of self-denial and sacrifice. At the beginning he had made daily visits to the poor, driving in his carriage, accompanied by his servants, but when he compared himself with his Master, he became convinced that he ought not to use the carriage and therefore decided to walk with a servant when performing these acts of charity. Finally, he even dismissed the servant and, unaccompanied, frequented the homes of the destitute, ministering to their needs.

Mingling with the poor he learned of the unemployment that was rife everywhere. In order to help them, he acquired a knowledge of those humble occupations which he might teach those in need of work and so help them become able providers for their families. In fact, he became so troubled over the wages of the lower working classes, that he even helped to form them into a union where they pooled the profits of their labors, taking what they needed for their own necessities and then sharing the remainder with the less fortunate among them. Had this practice been more universally accepted among the upper classes in France, the French Revolution might have been averted.

De Renty became convinced that apart from the Holy Spirit he could do nothing or say nothing which would eternally benefit his fellowmen. He would spend time in prayer before entering into conversation with them, fully expecting that the Holy Spirit Himself would speak through his lips. When the sick and poor began to come to his château from all directions, he would often gather them into his large dining room where he would first speak with them and then serve them with his own hands.

It was only natural that such conduct by one in his prominent position should invite abuse and misunderstanding from many quarters. It is not surprising that the most violent conflict was with his own mother, a thorough woman of the world, who considered her son's benefactions as totally indecorous. Her wish was that he would live in accordance with the demands of society and be controlled and governed by the protocol of those in higher positions of wealth.

It may have been that his arduous undertakings and personal oversight of so many seeking his help and counsel depleted his energies and shortened his life for he died at age thirty-seven. And it did not become easier toward the end. Gossips rumored that his godliness was all hypocrisy and that he was guilty of secret sins. There were those who delighted in spreading these rumors, and a religious community which owed him so much took the side of his adversaries. De Renty visited his betrayers and explained what had happened, but he records: "I met only with great humiliation. I took great care not to say a word to gain their favor. I spoke only what I owed to truth. For the rest I let all flow over me, disgrace and humiliation though it brought. I am outlawed here, or as the scapegoat in the Old Testament, driven into the wilderness."[2]

The humiliation was so great that for a time the Marquis kept to his room and did not enter upon his public duties. Troubles did not come singly, and soon he was bereaved of a daughter, then of his wife. He suffered still further through a painful illness which brought him very low. He writes:

> The pain I have is so great that I want to cry out and groan and lose control of myself. Though I feel it all the time, I can also say, my consciousness is with God and not with the pain. . . . Suffering is a gift, a great grace, but how rare a one. True, many suffer, but how few bear it in the way Christ did. It is strange, we know, that the only way in which He could enter His glory was the way of humiliation, agony, and the cross. Yet we, His disciples, are always desiring a different way from His. Is then the disciple above his Master?[3]

As his agony increased, he cried out, "Courage, courage! Eternity is drawing near!"[4] Those nearby heard his whisper, "I worship Thee! I adore Thee!" He knew that Jesus had established His Kingdom within him.

Although living for only thirty-seven years, the Marquis de Renty accomplished much in that brief time. John Wesley made over twenty references to him in his published letters, and in 1741, translated his life from German which he distributed to others. He rated this French nobleman along with the saintly Brainerd, encouraging his people to become acquainted with the lives of such godly characters in hope that they would be influenced to follow their example.

Stephen Grellet

FRENCH NOBLEMAN ON FOOT

It might well have been said that Stephen Grellet was born with a silver spoon in his mouth; in fact, it could have been a gold one, for every advantage favorable to a brilliant future surrounded his birth. Wealth was not wanting in the home into which Stephen was born on November 11, 1773. His father, a Roman Catholic, was a porcelain manufacturer as well as the proprietor of an iron works in Limoges, France. He was an intimate of Louis XVI and from him he had received a title of nobility because of his advances in the porcelain industry. He had also been comptroller of the Mint and at one time belonged to the household of Louis XVI, even attending his private chapel.

Stephen's mother, Susanne de Senamaud, had also brought prestige to the name of Grellet. Her ancestors had lived for generations in Limoges and the family was considered the most respected and aristocratic of all the families in that part of the country.

Two of Stephen's sisters had renounced the world, taking the veil and living behind convent walls in a very strict Roman Catholic order. Not so Etienne (later anglicized to Stephen), for he deeply thought out things for himself. "From my earliest days," he tells us, "there was that in me which would not allow me implicitly to believe the various doctrines I was taught. Though I was told that they were mysteries which I was not to seek to see into, yet my reasoning faculties brought me to the root of the matter; from created objects to the Creator⁻ from time to eternity."[1]

While studying in Lyons he had a parting of the veil which hides spiritual things from the natural man. This left a very deep impression. He says:

> I thought I saw a large company of persons, or rather purified spirits, on one of those floating vessels which they have at Lyons, on the Rhone, occupied by washerwomen. They were washing linen. I wondered to see what beating and pounding there was upon it, but how beautifully white it came out of their hands. I was told I could not enter God's kingdom until I underwent such an operation, that unless I was thus washed and made white, I could have no part in the dear Son of God. For weeks I was absorbed in the consideration of the subject⁻ the washing of regeneration. I had never heard of such things before, and I greatly wondered that, having been baptized with water, and having also received what they call the sacrament of confirmation, I should have to pass through such a purification; for I had never read or heard anyone speak of such a baptism.[2]

Through his teaching, Stephen had been led to expect that, during the rites of confirmation in the Roman Catholic Church, he would experience a change in his inner life and deportment. But what was his disappointment to find that "his sense of sin still remained, that his propensities to evil were that very day as strong as ever" and "thus," he adds, "at a very early age, I learned that neither priests nor Bishops could do the work for me."[3]

In spite of his early impressions and deep longings, his disillusionment with the Church of his childhood embittered him. And so his mind took a skeptical turn and he became a professed unbeliever. But his prayers and longings after God were soon to be answered though not, as is so often the case, in a manner exactly to his liking. Who would have thought that the advent of the French Revolution in 1789 would be used of the Lord in bringing Stephen to a place both spiritually and geographically where he would find Him Whom he had sought so long!

It was, of course, the nobility who felt the full venom of the Revolution. Many of the aristocrats fled, Stephen and his brother being among the number. Forced to leave their home, they wandered about in the woods and hills around Coblentz. Two or three times they just escaped death in a miraculous way before, at last, finding a refuge in America. Throughout these two years of turbulence, there had been this longing deep within him for purity and righteousness, but he had not yet found it in his heart to forego the pleasures of sense and time. An important crisis, however, was about to occur in Stephen Grellet's life which showed the Divine oversight of the youthful seeker. He describes it thus:

> Through adorable mercy, the visitation of the Lord was now again extended towards me, by the immediate openings of the Divine Light on my soul. One evening as I was walking in the field alone, my mind being under no kind of religious concern, nor in the least excited by anything I had heard or thought of, I was suddenly arrested by what seemed to be an awful voice proclaiming the words, "Eternity! Eternity! Eternity!" It reached my very soul; my whole man shook. It brought me, like Saul, to the ground. The great depravity and sinfulness of my heart was set open before me, and the gulf of everlasting destruction to which I was verging. I was made bitterly to cry out, "If there is no God, doubtless there is a hell." I found myself as in the midst of it. For a long time it seemed as if the thundering proclamation was yet heard. After that, I remained almost whole days and nights, exercised in prayer that the Lord would have mercy upon me, expecting that He would give me some evidence that He heard my supplication. . . .
>
> I now took up again the works of William Penn and opened upon *No Cross, No Crown*. The title alone reached to my heart. I proceeded to read it with the help of my dictionary,

having to look for the meaning of nearly every word. I read it twice through in this manner. I had never met with anything of the kind, neither had I felt the Divine Witness in me operating so powerfully before.

I now withdrew from company and spent most of my time in retirement and silent waiting upon God. I began to read the Bible with the aid of my dictionary for I had none then in French. I was much of a stranger to the inspired records. I had not even seen them before as I remember; what I had heard of any part of their contents was only detached portions in Prayer Books.

Whilst the fallow ground of my heart was thus preparing, my brother and myself, being one day at Colonel Corsa's, heard that a meeting for Divine Worship was appointed to be held next day in the Friends' Meeting House, by two English women on a religious visit to this land, to which we were invited. We felt inclined to go. The Friends were Deborah Darby and Rebecca Young. The sight of them brought solemn feelings over me; but I soon forgot the servants and all things around me; for, in an inward silent frame of mind, seeking for the Divine Presence, I was favored to find in me, what I had so long and with so many tears, sought for without me. . . . I felt the Lord's presence in such a manner, that my inner man was prostrated before my blessed Redeemer. . . . A secret joy filled me, in that I had found Him after Whom my soul had longed. I was as one nailed to my seat. . . .

My brother and myself were invited to dine in the company of these Friends at Colonel Corsa's. There was a religious opportunity after dinner, in which several communications were made. I could hardly understand a word of what was said, but, as D. D. began to address my brother and myself, it seemed as if the Lord opened my outward ear, and my heart. Her words partook of the efficacy of that "Word" which is "quick and powerful, and sharper than any two-edged sword." She seemed like one reading the pages of my heart, with clearness describing how it had been, and how it was with me. I was like Lydia: my heart was opened; I felt the power of Him Who hath the key of David. No strength to withstand the Divine visitation was left in me. . . . It was indeed a memorable day. I was like one introduced into a new world: the creation and all things around me bore a different aspect. My heart flowed with love to all. The awfulness of that day of God's visitation can never cease to be remembered with peculiar interest and gratitude, as long as I have the use of my mental faculties. I have been as one plucked from the burning⁻ rescued from the brink of a horrible pit.[4]

The new man in Christ was convinced that what had happened to him was not the fruit of his own imagination but the divine work of the Holy Spirit. We would call it the new birth, but that term is so lightly used at present in the religious world that it has lost much of its original meaning. Born of God! Born of the Spirit! Children of the Highest! Sons and daughters of God! What a tremendous, divine transformation!

The new convert felt the need for fellowship and found this among the Friends. Quakerism was under reproach in those days and as he was lodging with a Presbyterian family, he was warned about associating with a cult. His lack of courage in the face of such opposition caused him to forego the meetings for one Sunday.

Deep conviction seized him, however, and through the Holy Spirit's chiding, he decided to once again attend the assembly of the Quakers, but he took a circuitous route over fences and fields in order not to be seen. What was his chagrin to find there was no meeting that day, it having been transferred to a neighboring village. Finding the door closed, he sought a retired place to meditate. Here conviction for his great cowardice overwhelmed him. He felt like Nicodemus; he had sought to come to Jesus by night. God's disciplines were already beginning their fruitful work of stripping the new convert of all his own supposed goodness. Unknown to him as yet, he was being prepared to be a disciple who would eventually be called upon to venture further afield and find himself in situations where cowardice would indeed prove fatal.

Meanwhile, Stephen had taken a position as a teacher, and though being faithful to his profession, his mind was absorbed in the things of God. The verse, "Seek ye first the kingdom of God, and His righteousness; and all these things shall be added," was applied to his soul. His care for all temporal things was thus so handled by his faith in this promise that he felt at times he was almost not of this world. He gave himself without interval to meditation. "If I took a book," he says, "a single line would detain me for hours. Sometimes I have been a whole week in reading and pondering a single chapter in the Bible."[5]

We can trace the progressive steps in God's preparation of His worker in another lesson which He taught him from the Word about the necessity of having a concern for the souls of others:

> My mind was, at seasons, so taken up with a sense of the Lord's love, that it seemed as if I could have continued days and nights swallowed up in it. . . . Every step of my past life was retraced again and again. I suffered deeply not only for the evil I had done, but also for the good I had omitted to do, not only for the great loss I had sustained myself, but also for the harm I saw that my example might have done to others. I saw the emptiness and arrogance of Cain's reply to the Almighty, "Am I my brother's keeper?" We ought to be watchers over one another, and great is our responsibility as moral agents. The whole of God's creation, especially His national one, was brought very near to me. O! what is not the power of divine and redeeming love able to do?[6]

These testings of soul through which he passed during his early twenties he recalled in later years:

> He indeed led me about and instructed me, and brought me so under His discipline that in those days He was felt to be

the life of my soul, and the spring of my thoughts. The watch over the avenues of the heart was so maintained that if a single thought presented, foreign to heavenly things, or such as concerned not the salvation of my soul, I was greatly troubled; so that in the evening, when, as was my practice, before I made a record of the manner in which the day had been spent, I came, silently and solemnly, in the Lord's presence, to inspect my heart how it had been with it during the day. If I found that it had been turned, even for a short time, unprofitably from God, its center, I could not retire to rest, till I had a sense of the Divine mercy and forgiveness. My enquiry was not so much, whether I had retired from the world to wait upon God, as, whether I had retired from God's presence to harbor worldly thoughts. . . . My indwelling was then with the Lord, in His presence, at Whose school I learned, and in Whose discipline I was closely kept. . . . Many days and nights have I spent in pouring forth my tears before the Lord.[7]

At the age of twenty-five, three years after his conversion, the Divine call to service came to him with forcefulness. It was while yellow fever was raging in the city of Philadelphia where he resided. Many were dying and few wished to expose themselves to the ravages of this deadly plague. But Stephen Grellet felt he should visit the houses where death was devastating whole districts and pray with the dying. Many died in his presence, some evidencing great joy, peace, and fortitude; others "experienced the agony of death, throwing their arms around me to keep hold of a living object, crying out in bitterness, 'I cannot die! I am not fit to die!'"[8]

While nursing some Lascars who had taken the fever while their boat was in harbor, Grellet, himself, became the victim of the disease. The fever intensified; his extremities became cold, and his name was printed among the dead. A coffin was even prepared to receive his body for burial.

He tells in his own words what transpired in that moment:

Whilst death seemed to be approaching and I had turned myself on one side, the more easily, as I thought, to breathe my last, my spirit feeling already as encircled by the angelic host in the Heavenly Presence, a secret but powerful language was proclaimed on this wise: "Thou shalt not die, but live¯ thy work is not yet done." Then the corners of the earth, over seas and lands, were opened to me, where I should have to labor in the service of the Gospel of Christ. O what amazement I was filled with! What a solemn and awful prospect was before me! Sorrow took hold of me at the words, for it seemed as if I had already had a foot-hold in the Heavenly places. I wept sore, but, as it was the Divine will, I bowed in reverence before Him. . . . I saw and felt that which cannot be written. Suffice it to say that from that very time the disorder subsided.[9]

Being a man of decision, Stephen Grellet wasted no time in being about his Father's business. While visiting various parts of the States and Canada, he found many who were "the seed of the earth," a remnant scattered here and there. But he also deplored the drift he saw among the Quakers who had become materialistic and absorbed with the task of accumulating money.

It was during this period of six years of traveling over the American Continent that he met the woman who was to become his wife. He was now thirty-one years of age and he was to find in Rebecca Collins one who in every way would be a true help-mate. Throughout the years she proved a compatible companion who never held her husband back from his call even though it entailed many months and even years of separation. Even now that he was happily married, he would not allow a wife to keep him back from the Divine Mission. He knew God would take care of his loved one. And He did!

Shortly after his marriage, he was on one of his travels when he felt instinctively that he should return at once to his home in New York. The impression proved to have been from the Lord for he discovered that his mother-in-law had died of the plague and that his wife lay seriously ill of the same disease. Her health was, however, gradually restored, though it was some years before she recovered from the ill effects of this sickness.

Even though Rebecca was still in a poor state of health, the intensity of his call remained with him, urging him to be about his Master's business. Before leaving home once more, however, he received the promise, "My presence shall go with thee, and I will give thee rest." This comforted him many times in the days that followed.

"The steps of a good man are ordered by the Lord," the Bible says, and this was specially true of this foot-loose messenger of the Cross. Four times he crossed over to Europe, visiting palaces, prisons, and poor houses in England, Italy, Spain, France, Finland, Sweden, Russia, and Turkey. Greatly disturbed at what he found in the prisons, he would report the dreadful existing conditions and the many abuses practiced in these places to the monarchs who he felt were responsible for these social ills.

Wherever he went, Stephen Grellet found souls ready to harvest, and when his steps were directed to Haiti he preached to thousands of the military there. Then, when in Germany, he printed six thousand Bibles as he became aware of the great hunger for the Word of life.

While in London, he visited Newgate prison and was greatly agitated after seeing the condition of the women inmates. God used him to interest Elizabeth Fry on behalf of these unfortunate women and this became her life work.

Surely God's purposes are so much vaster than our small minds can grasp. Perhaps it will take eternity to reveal how much good this man of God did to the invisible Body of Christ scattered throughout the earth. These true members understood the man who understood the Almighty. He had no use for the hoary traditions, rites, and ceremonies of churches, long since bereft of life. He was cautious, however, about advising adherents as to what course of action they should take, having bold confidence in the Holy Spirit Who he knew could more ably guide them into all truth. He presented to them their rightful privilege in being kings and priests unto God, having the capacity of hearing personally from Him as to the way He would have them take.

And Grellet himself certainly availed himself of these privileges and if any man knew divine guidance it was he. If time and space permitted we would like to take you into the palaces where he was so wonderfully led and quote his own words as to the open doors set before him. He met many a noble princess in the Courts of Europe whose trust was simply in the Lord Jesus. At other times, the steps of this lonely ambassador would be guided to penetrate into convents and monasteries where he would meet nuns and priests who had received light beyond the dictates of their own church.

In Bavaria, he discovered a great company of priests who had found by revelation the kernel of true religion in a personal dependence upon Christ for their life. Though attached to an outward and visible organization, they had their roots in the Eternal. They had remained with the Church in order to influence the many sincere souls they had found there who would never see the light unless the heavy veil of formalism and traditionalism was lifted. When Stephen left, many souls had been strengthened who would otherwise have languished. To these he gave the Word of Life, tracts, or booklets which upon a second visit he would find had been used of God to further spiritual life in their souls.

In Russia, he was invited by the Archbishop into the seminary where he entreated the students to be aware of the influence of the Spirit of God "Who leads into all truth, by Whom alone the things of God can be known." When he took tea at the Archbishop's he found many priests and monks met together. He says:

Christ, the shepherd and bishop of souls, was preached to them; it is His prerogative to feed and instruct His people. His servants, even those who are divinely anointed as His ministers, can only hand out to the flock the bread which the Lord first gives them for the purpose, and which He Himself blesses. Neither can any availingly instruct the people but as the Lord Himself commissions and qualifies them by His Spirit so that they have nothing good to give but what they themselves first receive from the Divine fountain. Hence the necessity to attend to the dear Master's injunction to His disciples, "Tarry ye in the city of Jerusalem, until ye be endued with power from on high."[10]

From the accounts some may have of our often meeting with great and public characters, they may conclude that we ride about on the King's horse; but, from the exalted state in which Mordecai appeared placed, we saw and felt full well the humble station he must speedily assume. Though there is an outside washing and anointing, yet the sackcloth may remain underneath; and so to myself, I see little prospect of its being loosened from my loins, as long as I continue in this mutable state.

This Spirit-guided servant of the Lord sought to make no converts to his own denomination, allowing the Lord to add daily such as should be saved. He sought to build no church, recognizing the "My Church" which Jesus had spoken about; he sought to publish no statistics of converts. He was simply walking in the pathway of God, meeting the hungry and drawing out his soul to the afflicted.

Finally his path led the lone traveler on to Rome. He desired an audience with Pope Pius VII whose private secretary, Cardinal Consalvi, seemed to be favorably disposed toward him. We will better understand his mission from his own recording:

I was occupied very late last night in preparing the documents that Cardinal Consalvi wishes to have, relative to my visits to their public establishments. I apprehend it my duty to expose the various abuses that I have observed, and in several instances, misapplication of money designed for acts of benevolence. I represent also the sufferings of many of the prisoners in small, dark, crowded rooms and the heavy chains on them, which are not removed from some of them till after death.[11]

The courageous Quaker told the Cardinal many things which were faithfully relayed to the Pope. He spoke of his sadness of heart when he had heard "how the Bishop of Bavaria had hanged and burned the New Testament printed in Munich by Gossner, after the example of the Bishop of Naples, and how greatly this militates against Christianity."[12]

When he was granted an audience with the Pope, someone was stationed at the door to take the Quaker's hat so that the embarrassment and possibility of Grellet's retaining it upon entering the Pope's presence was thus removed. "I represented to him," Grellet writes, "what I had beheld in many places in Europe, and the West Indies, of the depravity and vices of many priests and monks, what a reproach they were to Christianity, and what corruption they are the means of spreading widely among the people. . . . I represented to him that Christ is the only Door, the only Savior. . . . In a kind and respectful manner he expressed a desire that 'the Lord would bless and protect me wherever I go.'"[13]

Stephen asked for permission to be shown the Inquisitorial Chambers. He gives details of his visit:

> These cells or small prisons, are very strongly built; the walls are of great thickness, all arched over. Some were appropriated to men, others to women. There was no possibility for any of the inmates to see or communicate with each other. The prison where Molinos was confined, was particularly pointed out. I visited also the prisons, or cellars

underground, and was in the place where the Inquisitor sat, and where tortures were inflicted on the poor sufferer; but everything bore marks that, for many years, these abodes of misery had not been at all frequented.

As we went on, I heard the Secretary say something to my interpreter about the *Secret Library*. I therefore asked him to take me there. He took me to the large Public Library. I told him this was not what I wished to see but the Secret One; he hesitated, stating that it was a secret place where there could be no admittance; that the priests themselves were not allowed to enter there.

I told him that the orders that had been read to him were to show me everything, that, if he declined to show me this, I might also conclude that he kept other places concealed from me; that therefore I could not contradict the reports I had heard, even in Rome, that the Inquisition was secretly conducted with the ancient rigor. On which he brought me into the *Secret Library*. It is a spacious place, shelved round up to the ceiling, and contains books, manuscripts, and papers condemned by the Inquisitors after they have read them. In the fore part of each book the objections to it are stated in general terms, or a particular page, and even a line is referred to, dated and signed by the Inquisitor, so that I could at once know the nature of the objection to any book on which I laid my hands.

The greater number of manuscripts appear to have been written in Ireland. Some of them contain very interesting matter, and evince that the writers, were, in many particulars learned in the school of Christ.

I could have spent days in that place. There are writings in all the various modern and ancient languages, European, Asiatic, Arabic, Grecian, etc., all arranged separately, in order. I carefully looked for Friends' books, but found none. There are many Bibles in the several languages; whole editions of some thousand volumes of the writings of Molinos.

After spending a long time in this place of much interest, the Secretary said, "You must now come and see my own habitation." I thought he meant the chamber that he occupies, but he brought me to spacious apartments where the archives of the Inquisition are kept, and where is the *Secretairerie.* Here are the records of the Inquisition for many centuries, to the present time.[14]

I find that monks, priests, and even Cardinals, are some of them under great excitement and irritation, highly offended at my having profaned their holy places, by inspecting their secret things in the Inquisition. The countenance that Consalvi has given me since my coming to Rome displeases them also. Some of them, I believe, are particularly sore, because I have exposed their misapplication of the money, intended, in several institutions, for acts of benevolence, and which they apply to their private use.[15]

I tread indeed among scorpions, but the Lord can deliver me out of all evil. I see no better way for me than to go straight forward in the path and line of service into which my blessed Lord directs me; the consequences I resign entirely to Him, as I have done also my life and my all.[16]

It is little wonder that this ambassador of Christ would come into conflict with the dogmas of the Roman Catholics for a true Quaker held extremely opposite views. As Grellet's biographer puts it:

They did not place any confidence whatever in the parade of external rites and ceremonies, the spurious aid of architectural display and the delusive charm of musical excitement; it lights no candles and burns no incense upon any visible altar, bows down to no graven image, adores no saint and recognizes no object of religious homage in the Virgin Mary.

Totally rejecting the notion of works of supererogation, it performs no pilgrimages to any sacred shrine, knows nothing of the miraculous power of relics, is an utter stranger to the imagined flames of purgatory, has no indulgences, no auricular confession, no sacerdotal absolution, no masses for the living, no prayers for the dead. It acknowledges no mediator between God and man but Christ, no justification of the sinner but through faith in His blood, no sanctification of the believer but by His Spirit. It has no sacraments but that of the washing of regeneration⁻ the baptism of the Holy Ghost and fire, and that of participation by faith, in the body and blood of our Lord Jesus Christ, the Savior of the world⁻ no hope of eternal life but through the one offering whereby He has perfected for ever them that are sanctified.

The Quakers believed their Head was Christ Who was Ruler over the Church, and each member of that Body was a king and priest in his own right. They so honored the Person of the Holy Spirit that they felt no human authority should conflict with the guidance of the individual member. They did not believe that a paid ministry was Scriptural. The true Church, they maintained, did not consist of only one denomination, but of all true born-again believers who had been baptized into the Body of Christ.

Looking back in retrospect upon this time of traveling, Stephen Grellet never repined over the hardships or separations from home and family but said:

The fields in many parts I have visited are white unto harvest, so that sometimes I have wished that I might have the life of Methuselah, or that the sun might never go down, that I might do my share of that great work which is to be done in these nations. There is a most precious seed in these parts, and in places where I have not actually visited. . . .

I have been with rich and poor, princes and princesses, Protestant ministers and Popish priests, all speaking but one language, not upholding forms and ceremonies, but Christ and His Spirit. I have visited various of those Romish priests in Bavaria of whom we had heard, and have found them to be spiritually minded men. I am nearly united to some of them. A few have married, and have answered those who have come to visit them on that account out of the Scriptures, and the practice of the primitive church, and they continue Romish priests still, much beloved by the people, among whom they exercise a good influence. Many of the people desire to have the Scriptures but have it not yet in their power to obtain them.[17]

How outstanding was this man's faith in the individual guidance of the Spirit! Just because many have abused this privilege of the Christian and gone into fanaticism, is no reason why we should abandon this Scriptural right of the believer. "As many as are led by the Spirit of God, **they are the sons of God.**" It is so easy for impatient flesh to step ahead of God when the waiting becomes tedious. Our God is never in a hurry. But there is a pathway in the sea of humanity where we might trace the footsteps of God. As the hymn writer puts it, "He plants His footsteps in the sea." Those footsteps will inevitably lead His servants who follow Him to those obscure and hidden places of the earth where hungry-hearted humanity exists, for "the eyes of the Lord run to and fro throughout the whole earth, to show himself strong in the behalf of them whose heart is perfect toward him."

It was to these perfect in heart that Grellet was so often led in most wonderful ways. He believed that there was perfect timing in the Spirit's guidance. Had not Christ said to His own brethren when they urged Him to go up to the feast, "My time is not yet come: but your time is alway ready"? As natural men, their wills were not controlled by the Spirit of God and they could not understand Jesus submitting all His plans to His heavenly Father. But His disciples, after yielding their wills entirely to God at Pentecost and being baptized into the Body of Christ, were divinely led to those in desperate need: Ananias to Saul of Tarsus; Philip the evangelist, from his scheduled revival meetings in Samaria to the Ethiopian eunuch in the lone desert way; Peter to Cornelius; Paul to Lydia at the seaside. Jesus Christ, the divine Head, directs His unseen Body in just the same way that the brain, from its numerous nerve centers, co-ordinates the human body making it function harmoniously.

Stephen Grellet knew his God. He was thoroughly convinced that only the Spirit's guidance would lead him to reap where the grain was ready to harvest. "My mind," he tells us, "has been under great concern that I might have a clear sense of the right way in which I am now to proceed on this important embassy of my great Lord and Master; for I believe that there is **a right time and place for every day's work,** and my earnest desire is, that, day by day, I may be thus found engaged in serving the Lord. He has condescended now to renew with clearness the impressions I had whilst in America."

He often found hunger in unexpected places. When visiting his elderly mother who had come to know God personally since he had last seen her, he met an aged Mother Superior at a nearby hospital of whom he writes:

> I found that, Cornelius-like, she wished that her household should share with her in the consolations she hoped for from my visit. She therefore had all the nuns collected. We were soon brought into solemn silence before the Lord, Who baptized us together "by the one Spirit into the one body." Then was my heart enlarged among them on the love of Christ Who was preached to them as the only Savior. . . . That baptism which constitutes the new creature was set before them, and also the Bread of Life, on which this new-born child of God lives. As he is not born of man, nor of the will of man, but of God, so none of the doings or workings of man can minister living bread to him but Christ alone, even through faith in His Name.[18]

Writing of a visit Grellet made to Bavaria, Grellet's biographer tells us: "Three weeks had now been spent in the midst of a body of Christians in Bavaria, who, in the bosom of the Roman church, fully confessed by their faith and practice the grand fundamental principles of the Reformation. The bold and unflinching testimony thus borne against many of the leading tenets and corruptions of Rome, had been attended with a large measure of blessing both to priests and people."[19]

Throughout the years, Grellet met some of the prominent men we read of in Church History‾ Stilling, Sailer, Boos, Tholuck, Gossner, and many others too numerous to mention here. Of some visits he said: "Our religious intercourse was truly pleasant. My spirit is often contrited when meeting here and there with the Lord's visited children, who, like a little salt, are sprinkled over the land. If these are faithful in their several allotments, they may be like lights in the world."

He speaks in particular of a General Stockhorn who "was in a very broken state of mind, strong are the convictions of the Spirit of Truth upon him," and of a Baroness Drudener whom he describes as "a remarkable woman . . . an instrument of real good among several young women of high rank, particularly here at court." It was the burden of his heart to direct these searching souls to the teachings of the Lord's Spirit in their own hearts, telling them that, to hear the language of the Spirit, silence on our part and cessation from our own actings is necessary; we must "hearken and hear what the Lord has to say unto us."[20]

At one time he met the Archbishop from Finland with whom he shared his thoughts of the futility of many of the ceremonies and practices which have found a place among different religious denominations and for which there is little authority in the Holy Scriptures. And once, when visiting Russia, he commented:

> We went to see Princess Metchersky. She is a woman of superior mental abilities, greatly improved and directed to the right channel for usefulness by the grace and Spirit of the Lord Jesus Christ. . . . She was an instrument in the Lord's hands in fostering religious impressions in the mind of the Emperor, when he first came under the powerful convictions of the Spirit of Truth. As a proof that the Emperor is in the daily practice of reading the Scriptures, she states to us that

some years since they agreed to begin to read the Bible at the same time, one chapter of the Old Testament in the morning, and another of the New Testament in the evening. . . . He wishes her to translate and print the excellent work of William Penn, called, *No Cross, No Crown*; believing that it would be highly beneficial, especially to those of high rank in the Empire. Our next visit was to the Minister of the Interior; his wife is seriously disposed, as also appears to be the Princess Shabatoff, who resides with them.[21]

Grellet was always aware of the cost of such a ministry. "Many baptisms," he writes, "has the Christian to endure; may those that I pass through purify my soul, and prepare me for the Lord's service, whether it be actively to do, or silently to suffer His Divine will."[22]

Oh what an amazing thing it is for the Christian worker to desist from his own labors and enter into the rest of God! This does not mean inactivity, but activity directed to effectual and eternal benefits. Listen to Grellet once more: "Amidst the thick clouds of darkness that hang over the nations, and the tumult of war, there are here and there those who know the Lord Jesus to be their sanctuary. My spirit was refreshed in a meeting with a company of these pious persons when the external hardships of the preceding nights were forgotten."

It is reasonable to expect that such extensive travels would need financing. Stephen Grellet was only too aware of this and met his own financial needs through a business he owned in New York and there would be times when he would attend to this business in order to not be chargeable to any man for his travels. The result was that he even had enough at times to help those in distress.

We have not enumerated the hardships of the way ̄ the dangers from pirates on the sea, and bandits on lonely mountain roads. The elements at times were battled fiercely. Sometimes snow would lie heavily in his path, or heavy rain make the crossing of swollen rivers hazardous. Very little did Grellet make of these difficulties and God brought his travels abroad largely to an end in his sixty-ninth year, although he was still able to make shorter trips and lived to the old age of eighty-two.

Stephen Grellet passed to his reward on November 16, 1855, saying: "My heart and my strength faileth but . . . do not be discouraged; it is only the flesh."[23]

For sixty years he had faithfully served God Who had called him. He could truthfully say with Paul, that he had finished his course for he had traveled over 28,000 miles when the modes of travel were very primitive. He had brought the Light of Life to many who had sat in darkness. He had ministered nourishment to the members of Christ's body wherever the Divine Guide had led his footsteps.

We wish to close with an incident related in a Quaker magazine which strikingly showed the marvelous way in which Stephen Grellet understood and followed God's guiding hand:

> Stephen Grellet, after much waiting on the Lord to show him His will, was directed by the Spirit to take a long journey into the backwoods of America and preach the Gospel to some wood-cutters who were felling the forest timber. The Spirit-guided man went his lonely journey in great peace and joy of soul, and went direct to the place told him of in his prayers.
>
> He found a number of shanties, but to his surprise there was silence. The timber-cutters had gone away deeper into the forest. But he who had his message from God could not be deceived. Finding a large shanty that appeared to have been used for the meals of the men, he entered, stood up, and preached the everlasting Gospel, finished, and returned supremely happy in having done the will of his Father in Heaven.
>
> Years passed away, and Stephen Grellet heard nothing of his visit in any way, but he was happy in knowing that he had followed the Holy Spirit's guidance. He came to Europe

in the service of the Gospel and visited England. One day, walking across London Bridge, a man somewhat rudely took hold of him, with "I have found you at last; I have got you at last, have I?"

"Friend," said Stephen Grellet, "I think thou art mistaken."

"But I am not," said the man. After many more exclamations on the one hand and replies from the servant of the Lord on the other, the stranger said, "Did you not preach on a certain day and at a certain place in the backwoods of America?"

"Yes," said the good man, "but I saw no one there to listen."

"I was there," was the reply. "I was the ganger of the woodmen. We had moved forth into the forest, and were putting up more shanties to live in, when I discovered that I had left my lever at the old settlement. So after setting my men to work I had gone back alone for my instrument. As I approached the old place, I heard a voice. Trembling and agitated, I drew near, saw you thro' the chinks of the timber walls of our dining shanty, listened to you, and was deeply convinced of sin, but I left and went back to my men. The arrow stuck fast. I was miserable, miserable for many weeks. I had no Bible, no book of any kind, no one to speak to about Divine things.

"Ah! my men were grossly immoral. I felt more and more wretched. At last I possessed myself of the sacred treasure. I read and read till I read words whereby I obtained eternal life. I told my men the same blessed news, and they were all converted to God. Three of them became missionaries and were mightily used of the Holy Spirit to bring sinners to the Savior, and," added the strange man, "I became possessed of the very strong desire to see you and tell you that I knew that your sermon in our old quarters had been the means of the conversion of at least one thousand souls."

Surely God moves in a mysterious way His wonders to perform![24]

Samuel Pearce

THE BRAINERD OF THE BAPTISTS

When a man sets out to fulfill the call of God, the Almighty sets in motion the machinery of Heaven. It may often be so imperceptibly and so silently accomplished that it is scarcely noted except when seen in retrospect from a higher plateau.

William Carey is well known as a pioneer in foreign missions, but his supporters are perhaps not so well known. When he was fired with a zeal to make the world his parish, he was surrounded by four godly men who undertook to raise finance for him, and, more than that, to hold the ropes in prayer while he set out to pioneer foreign missions. As the years passed, these stalwarts remained true to their promise to support this courageous pioneer. As long as Carey could depend upon these godly men, much given to communion, his work was well represented at home. But when they passed on to be with God, and a new committee was appointed, grave misunderstandings existed between the Home Committee and the missionaries in India, causing much distress to those on the field.

These four men, Pearce, Fuller, Sutcliffe, and Ryland, burned with zeal to promote the spread of the Gospel in heathen lands. And while each of them was remarkable for piety, Samuel Pearce was perhaps the most outstanding. He was not only the pastor of a large parish in Birmingham, England and was considered a prince among preachers, but his intense prayer-life and spiritual sensitivity earned him the title: "Brainerd of the Baptists."

Samuel Pearce was born July 20, 1766, at Plymouth in the south of England. His father was a silversmith with a considerable business. Samuel's mother died at the time of his birth, and so he was taken care of in the home of his grandfather who was very fond of the motherless boy who was never strong. Between the ages of eight and ten Samuel was taken back into the home of his own father, who had doubtless remarried. He wished the boy to become his assistant, for business was brisk and helpers were needed.

When the lad was about sixteen, a young student minister, Isaiah Birt, came to preach at the church where Samuel worshiped. Describing his own experience of salvation under this youthful preacher, he says: "I believe few conversions were more joyful. The change produced in my views, feelings, and conduct was so evident to myself, that I could no more doubt of its being from God than of my existence. I had the witness in myself and was filled with peace and joy unspeakable."

His biographer said of this dynamic experience: "All the attractions of his godless associates vanished. He was Christ's war-prize, led captive into the harbor of God's will, and in his new captivity, finding himself free."

Writing to his spiritual father Samuel pleaded: "Never forget me. Oh, beseech of God that He will ever keep me from a lukewarm, a Laodicean spirit! May my affections to the crucified Savior be continually on a flame! Religion makes a beggar superior to a king! What can equal the felicity of a Christian⁻ the soul's calm sunshine and the heart-felt joy? Nothing! Nothing!"

Samuel was to be nurtured in a church that had previously been brought through great tribulation. Some had been flung into prison and then banished. One so imprisoned said: "A week in prison giveth plainer discovery of a man's spirit than a month in church."

When only nineteen, he was voted by his fellow church members to be set apart to preach. It was evident to them that the boy should be given further training, and as the Plymouth Baptist Church had always been associated with the Bristol Education Society, it was to Bristol that young Pearce was sent. Here he became acquainted with Robert Hall, a former Bristol student.

Samuel joined himself in prayer sessions with several others who were ardent lovers of Jesus Christ and it became evident that he was already embarking upon a life of prayer. "I hope you will still be cautious in your intimacies," he writes in a letter to an Edinburgh medical student. "You will gain more by a half-hour's intercourse with God than the friendships of the whole College can impart."

When it came to leaving college, Samuel felt as though he were leaving the safe harbor for the open sea. "I was sorry," he wrote later, "to leave my studies to embark, inexperienced as I am, on the tempestuous ocean of public life, where the high blowing winds and rude noisy billows must inevitably annoy the trembling voyager."

Many souls were won to God during Samuel Pearce's pastoral years, but this did not mean that he escaped the prophetic warning Christ gave to His followers: "All that will live godly in Christ Jesus shall suffer persecution." In his zeal to keep the church pure, he used a discipline, a vigilance, and a constancy in calling others to consecration and service which were not too well received by his parishioners. For six months, the peace of the church was disturbed by their open opposition. There were many censures and there came a day when two ring-leaders were openly expelled. The church then united in heart-searching and increased prayer, meeting for intercession every week-day at five o'clock and four or five times on the Sabbath. This continued for two weeks. During Pearce's ministry in this church, there were over 300 new members. He writes:

I have borne the most positive testimony against the prevailing evils of professing Christians of this city: sensuality, gaiety, vain amusements, neglect of the Sabbath; and last night I told an immense crowd of these of the first rank that if they made custom and fashion their plea, they were awfully deluding their souls. Yesterday morning from Psalms 5:7 I seriously warned them against preferring their bellies to God, and their own houses to His. . . . Never, never did I feel more how weak I am in myself, and how strong in the omnipotence of God. I feel a superiority to all fear, and possess a conscious dignity in being an ambassador of Christ.

Pearce's biographer gives us this further insight into his character:

Clearly this gentle lamb could be a lion. He could twist the cords into a whip. He could lay the axe to the tree roots. His voice could be "stormy in men's ears." Nevertheless he was a very prince of courtesy towards all of different convictions from his own. He had a strong distaste for controversy. When he was compelled to draw the sword, he at least kept it clean of all malice.

Pearce's passion for the Christly life was the secret of all his influence. Upon his face men caught the light that shone on Moses and Stephen. They knew he practiced God's presence, that God could whisper in his ear, that he dared to be God's friend. "Inly his spirit to God's silence listened." He felt that he had built his booth upon the holy mount, not for the tarrying of any prophet but for the sole abiding of his Lord. His chief solicitude was for the culture of the Holy Ghost. "Oh, for more of Enoch's spirit!" he kept crying. "May I know more and more the blessing of the beloved disciple," was his abiding prayer⁻ the very prayer which was richly answered for those who knew him best entitled him just that⁻ the beloved disciple.

He writes: "I want more heart religion⁻ I want a more habitual sense of the Divine Presence. I want to walk with God." "There is nothing that grieves me so much or brings such darkness on my soul, as my little spirituality and frequent wanderings in secret prayer. I cannot neglect the duty; but it is seldom I enjoy it." "I feel the little advance I have made; more light to be sure, I have; but light without heat leaves the Christian half dissatisfied." "A few seasons of spirituality I have enjoyed, but my inconstant heart is too prone to rove from its proper center."

He longed to "abide, like the planet Mercury, close to the central sun." "Oh for more supplies from the exhaustless mines of grace!" One early Lord's Day morning he wrote:

> "I read that He, on duty bent,
> To lonely places often went,
>   To seek His Father there;
> The early morn and dewy ground
> Could witness they the Savior found
>   Engaged in fervent prayer.
>
> "And was my Savior wont to pray
> Before the light unveiled the day,
>   And shall I backward be?
> No! dearest Lord, forbid the thought,
> Help me to fight, as Jesus fought,
>   Each foe that hinders me."

For one so young to be so talented and gifted with preaching abilities was no small snare but to be aware of our dangers is the first guard against becoming entrapped. Samuel realized his temptation to pride and guarded against it. "I am ashamed," he wrote to Ryland, "that I have so much pride. I want more and more to become a little child, to dwindle into nothing in my esteem, to renounce my own wisdom, power, and goodness, and to simply live upon Jesus for all."

He further mourned this tendency to exaltation in a letter to his wife: "My thirst for preaching Christ, I fear, abates; and a detestable vanity for the reputation of a good preacher, as the world terms it, has already cost me many conflicts." And to

Carey, he confides: "Flattering prospects of reputation and wealth have had too much ascendancy over me." But later, when consecrating his life to India as one of toil and few benefits, he wrote in his diary: "All prospects of pecuniary independence and growing reputation, with which in unworthier moments I had amused myself, were chased from my mind; and the desire of living wholly to Christ swallowed up every other thought."

Samuel Pearce was most fortunate that in his wife he found someone to whom he could unbosom his heart without reserve. When she lay near death's door at the birth of her first child, Pearce went through great agony of soul, saying, "I shall never fear another trial. He that sustained me amidst the flame will defend me from every other spark. Oh, my Sarah, had I as much proof that I love Jesus Christ as I have of my love to you, I should prize it more than rubies."

Meanwhile a call came to Carey, Fuller, and Ryland, all members of the Northampton Association of Baptist Ministers, to awaken a sleeping Britain to the vast fields untouched as yet by the Gospel. When we remember that there were few missionaries abroad at the time of which we are here speaking, we conclude that the stepping out upon such a venture would be fraught with many misgivings by staid, formal Church-members and dignitaries. Indeed, Carey and his associates encountered great indifference to the cause of foreign missions.

This indifference, however, did little to daunt William Carey. He wrote a pamphlet which was widely distributed on the duty of obeying God's command to "go into all the world and preach the Gospel." And when he preached his eventful sermon on "Expect great things from God; attempt great things for God," he tried to prove the "criminality of the Church's supineness in the cause of God." Ryland had been so moved that, after listening to this impassioned appeal, he wondered that all the people did not respond unanimously. When, however, all were quietly leaving the assembly room without anything being done, Carey wrung the hand of his friend, Fuller, and said in anguish, crying aloud, "Is nothing again to be done?" Hearing the distressed cry of Carey, the people returned and it was agreed to have a meeting of the Association which would be at Kettering.

Although Samuel Pearce had not been a member of the Northampton Association and knew the ministers but little, he made his way to that eventful October meeting at Kettering in which it was decided to form the Baptist Missionary Society. Someone writing of this meeting, describes it thus: "He (Christ) was 'coming again' into His Church that evening (in Kettering), initiating vast world-conquests, when He burned in the hearts of those humble pastors gathered in Widow Wallis's parlor, and moved them to both dare and to give. He did not cry, nor cause His voice to be heard in the streets. He blew no trumpet before Him. The busy world took no note of that little Kettering company. Nevertheless it was of prodigious import, and its line has gone out through all the earth, and its impulse to the end of the world."

God does indeed choose the weak things, and the beginning of foreign missions in Britain had nothing of special note to mark it as far as worldly wisdom would demand. Apart from the four⁻ Sutcliffe, Pearce, Fuller, and Ryland⁻ the other members were "merest ciphers, as the world would reckon⁻ village pastors of no fame and of scantiest salary." Pearce's biographer said of the fifteen men who formed the first Baptist Missionary Society, "Three fourths of them were nobodies from 'nowheres,' from petty Nazareths. What weight could their names carry in the rest of the Denomination? Had London now and its Baptist Leaders originated the movement, there might have been a hope of general confidence and support, but they considered their own feebleness and were persuaded that He Who was calling them was 'able also to perform.'"

The inception of the Christian Church had taken place in a similar fashion. There was little or no stir when the Messiah came on that night long ago to an obscure village of Palestine. Silently the young mother took the young Babe and walked in unannounced to the temple, and only those whose ears were attune to Heaven knew that a momentous event was taking place. By the Holy Ghost, two aged persons came into the temple and beheld the Babe, and prophesied. Silently He grew up in Nazareth making no great hue and cry about His years of preparation. Silently He had left the wondering disciples, and but for them, Jerusalem would never have known about the ascension. So He always comes, and "the history of the Church is the verification of the prophecy, for He has ever come most mightily in this unobserved fashion."

Pearce preached to his people the next Sunday relating the happenings of that Kettering meeting, and they formed the first Auxiliary Society, and soon gathered £70 for the cause of Carey. That was quite a sum if we remember that the minister's salary was only £100 a year.

At the next meeting of the Missionary Society, Dr. Thomas, a former ship's surgeon who knew India's needs because he had served there as lay minister, was invited to be present. And so Carey and his friends decided to make India their mission field. Later, in January, Dr. Thomas and William Carey were appointed as the Society's first missionaries. At a meeting in November, Dr. Thomas was eager to have a colleague to go out with him, and this was taken as a token of Divine direction. Acquaintance with Dr. Thomas had led Carey and his friends to think seriously of India as their first mission field. Pearce and Carey, overjoyed, embraced one another.

In the years that followed, these four men⁻ Pearce, Fuller, Ryland, and Sutcliffe⁻ never failed to give their last measure of devotion. Carey had asked them to hold the ropes and he would venture down the mines to explore the wealth. "Holding the ropes," however, proved to be no mean task. We, who live in days when foreign missions have been in progress and accepted for many years as an integral part of the Church's obligation, find it hard to realize how untried these paths were to these first invaders for Christ. When appealing to people to do away with superfluities and luxuries in order to give to such a worthy enterprise, Pearce said he often got "only beggars' fare," and Fuller would "sometimes retire from the public streets into the back lanes that he might not be seen to weep for his so little success."

Yet it is amazing with what untiring vigor these men pursued their goal to interest the public in the financial needs of the two pioneers. Fuller's grandson commented: "They were as familiar with the highways to London and with all the roads of Mid-England as postmen are with their rounds." When we remember that the automobile was not as yet in use and that the roads were atrocious, and stage coaches infrequent, we can realize a little of the toils of the road which these eager servants of God endured.

It was over a year after the departure of the two missionaries before the committee heard of their safe arrival. Meanwhile, Samuel Pearce grew more restless because he himself wished to go out to India and join his friend Carey. For a period of some months his diary recorded his intense longing to be considered worthy to go abroad as God's herald.

During this time of waiting, Pearce's spiritual life deepened as he consecrated to God for a life with no certain income, and one which entailed the hazards of venturing with his wife and children into an unfriendly climate. A diary extract will reveal his deepening grasp of God's purposes:

> At a prayer-meeting tonight felt crucifixion to the world, disesteem for all it holds. . . . Frowns and smiles, fullness and

want, honor and reproach, now equally indifferent. When closing the meeting, my whole soul felt as if it were going after the lost sheep of the heathen. I long to raise my Master's banner where the sound of His fame hath scarcely reached.

Reread my diary. My heart much more fixed. . . . Much struck in 2 Corinthians 1 with the piety of Paul in not purposing after the flesh; the seriousness of spirit with which he formed his designs, and his steadfast adherence to them. Read David Brainerd's life up to the time of his missionary appointment. The exalted devotion of that dear man made me question mine. Yet at some seasons he speaks of sinking as well as rising.

Seemed without prayer power. All was dullness, when on a sudden God smote the rock with the rod of His Spirit, and immediately the waters flowed. What a view of the love of a crucified Redeemer! I was as a giant refreshed with new wine; like Mary, at the Master's feet, for tenderness of soul; like a little child, for submission; and like Paul, for victory over all self-love. An irresistible drawing of soul which far exceeded anything I ever felt before, and which can never be described nor conceived by those who have never experienced it, all constrained me to vow, that I would, by His leave, serve Him among the heathen. The Bible lying open before me, on my knees, many passages caught my eye, and confirmed the purpose of my heart. If ever in my life I knew anything of the Holy Spirit, I did then. I was swallowed up in God. Christ was all in all. Many times I concluded prayer, but was sweetly drawn back to it till my physical strength was almost exhausted. The more I am thus, the more I pant for the service of my blessed Master among the heathen.

These outbreathings show with what animation the heart leaped to the thought of going abroad, but his friends opposed his going, and Fuller, whom he revered, brought up many objections. A letter followed also from Ryland stating his objections. "If my brethren knew," Pearce explained, "how earnestly I pant for the work, they could not withhold their ready acquiescence."

Fuller informed the committee of Samuel Pearce's resolve to go to India, if his brethren would give their consent. He told them he had asked that a day of fasting and prayer be set aside for this purpose. They fixed the date and place of the meeting⁻ November 12 at Northampton. These men spent the morning fasting and praying together. Pearce presented his position to his brethren. His diary was not read then because it was too long, but after his death, when the committee read the deep passionate longings, they wondered whether or not they had made a wrong decision.

At two o'clock Pearce and his deacon-friends withdrew and gave themselves to more intense prayer, while the Committee deliberated. For almost two hours they conferred, till unanimously they decided adversely. The group concluded: "His learning, piety, character, and popular abilities promise to render him (Pearce) one of the first ministers of the denomination. I admire the disinterestedness, ardor, and magnanimity of his soul, though he should never go."

Pearce accepted their verdict with meekness: "One thing I have resolved⁻ if I cannot go abroad I will do all I can to serve the Mission at home. . . . I do not care where I am, whether in England or in India, so that I am employed as He would have me; but surely we need pray hard that God would send more help to Hindustan."

He wrote letters of assurance and comfort to Carey. "Do not fear the want of money. I will travel from Land's End to the Orkneys but we will get money enough for all the demands of the Mission. . . . Men we only want; and God shall find them for us in due time."

Over in India, Carey had felt the impact of a day set apart by the Home Committee for special prayer. These faithful warriors rejoiced when William Ward, the young printer and newspaper-editor whom Carey had met formerly at Hull, volunteered to go. When Pearce had been laid aside by illness, he had written to Ward, then a theological student, asking him to come and fill his pulpit for a month. And Ward was thus given an intimate knowledge of the man who held the ropes so admirably.

Writing later of Pearce, Ward said, "Oh, how does personal religion shine in Pearce! What a soul! What ardor for the glory of God! What diffusive benevolence toward all, especially towards all who love Christ, and who show it by their devotion to His will. Instead of being all froth and fume, you see in him a mind wholly given up to God; a sacred luster shines in his conversation; always tranquil, always cheerful. It is impossible to doubt the reality of religion if you are acquainted with Pearce. I have seen more of God in him, than in any other person I ever met."

Samuel Pearce was doubtless Carey's most frequent correspondent, and his letters showed that his heart was truly still in India: "Long as I live, my imagination will be hovering over you in Bengal; and should I die, if spirits are allowed a visit to the world they have left, mine would soon be at Mudnabatty, watching your labors, your conflicts, and your pleasures."

What praying these men did! Was their associate ill? A day would be spent in intercession on his behalf. Was there a decision to make? A day of fasting and prayer would soon bring order out of chaos. Ward writing to Pearce said: "We four missionaries and brothers Fuller and Sutcliffe, are going into an upper room this evening to pray and to commemorate our Savior's death."

In a letter written by Pearce to his congregation whom he had served for ten years, he confides:

> The only way to be constantly happy is to be constantly looking to and coming to a Crucified Savior; renouncing all our own worth; cleaving to Him for all; giving up everything

that clashes with our fidelity to Him; receiving from His fullness "grace upon grace"; relying on His every promise, and guarding against aught that might for a moment bring distance and darkness between our souls and our Lord.

Pearce's health began to show signs of deterioration in 1793, but in spite of this, he would rally and take up once again the heavy loads. When after an arduous day, he would sit up by night learning Bengali and studying up on Missions, a toll was being taken which would unexpectedly end this useful life. Doubtless, too, he had inherited a weakened constitution from his mother who had died at his birth. Yet few thought his life was endangered; Fuller's health had given concern for all, but the Mission regarded Pearce to be "labor-proof and weather-proof for at least another thirty years."

When riding back from Kettering in October, however, he took a chill that made him a sufferer for twelve months, and terminated in his death. He could scarce speak with a friend without losing his breath. He wrote: "What a mercy that my health has not been impaired by vice; but that, on the contrary, I am bearing in my body the marks of the Lord Jesus. . . . Oh sweet affliction! I would not have been without it for the Indies; it has taught me more of my Bible and my God than seven years' study could have done."

A warmer climate was advocated, and Pearce left his wife and five children to go to his father in Plymouth. Mr. Pearce Sr. immediately grasped the seriousness of the situation when he noticed the deterioration in his son's health.

Rarely have we found men so godly, so prayerful, and so loving to one another as were these four men and their missionary colleagues in India. When William Ward heard of Pearce's illness he wrote: "Oh, my God! What would I give for a restoration to health of Brother Pearce! Oh, if it be possible, spare⁻ oh, spare his precious life! If I could have walked on the water, I would have made long strides to Plymouth tonight and laid his dear, aching head upon my throbbing heart."

Fuller was also heart-stricken at the prospect of losing his dear friend and prayer-partner as the following quotation reveals:

> Fuller rarely wept, for he was of vigorous brain more than of tearful heart. Not that he lacked tenderness. His granite was not without its moss. . . . There were deep wells of tenderness in this sturdy soul. . . . 1st of June he could not stay his tears, for none were losing more than he. He knew, better than others, what a pillar of the Mission Pearce had ever been— how strong and how beauteous. He had no other comrade so like-minded. Indeed, Pearce's ardor had often kept his own soul aglow. It was as though Peter was losing John. Never had Fuller ridden the seventy miles from London to Kettering with such foreboding. By the calendar it was the first of June; by his spirit, it was the depth of December. He tells us that "thinking of that dear man Pearce wasting away at Plymouth, he was overcome for miles together weeping." Nevertheless, before he reached Kettering, his grief had been chastened into prayer and of that praying, this, he says, was the sum, "Let the God of Samuel Pearce be my God."

Though very ill, and not responding to the southern clime, the sick man returned homeward but not before spending five days with the Ryland's. Another stop-over was managed at his wife's home where her sisters lovingly cared for the invalid. It was July 19 when he at last reached Birmingham to be in the midst of his own family. He had had to take twelve days to travel from Plymouth to Birmingham. His wife moaned when she saw his changed appearance but with her he found a Chamber of Peace.

As he faced death, his submission to Christ's will was most apparent. "Oh, what a satisfying thought it is," he tells us, "that God does appoint those means of dissolution, whereby He gets most glory to Himself! Of all the ways of dying, that which I have dreaded most was by consumption. But my dear Lord, if by this death I can glorify Thee, I prefer it to all others."

A week later and much weaker, the dying man confessed: "My voice is gone, so that I cannot whisper without pain, and of this I am at times most ready to complain. For to see my dear wife look at me, and then at the children, at length bathe her face in tears, without my being able to say one kind word of comfort! Yet the Lord supports me under this also; and I trust He will to the end."

As the disease progressed, writing was an impossibility. Scorched with fever, he managed to whisper, "Hot, yet happy." After a severe coughing spell, he said, "If I ever recover, I shall pity the sick more than ever." After a restless night, he pled, "Only pray that I may have patience. I fear I dishonor God by impatience. My sick bed has been my Bethel."

October 10 was the day of his release from pain to the presence of God. Before going, however, his wife noticing that the end was near, repeated to him the last verse of Newton's hymn:

"Since all that I meet shall work for my good,
The bitter is sweet; the medicine, food;
Though painful at present, 'twill cease before long,
And then, oh, how pleasant the conqueror's song."

He caught the final phrase and with a smile repeated it⁻ "the conqueror's song." "In a few minutes" his biographer tells us, "he was gone⁻ leaving autumn behind him for perpetual spring, and the Paradise of God." He was but thirty-three years of age. It would be ten months before Carey would hear of the decease of his beloved Pearce. When Fuller heard of his death, he wrote to his wife, "Memoirs of his life must be published;

he is another Brainerd." Later when Ryland wrote a life of Pearce he termed him "The Seraphic."

Pearce's widow survived him by only five years, having buried their youngest son Samuel a short time after her husband's death. And what of the children? William Hopkins Pearce was only ten years old at his father's death. He got an excellent training in the printing trade, but what was more important, he learned about the Saviorhood of Christ. He felt drawn to India as had his father. For twenty-three years he labored in Calcutta, founding and making self-supporting the Baptist Mission Press.

Pearce's second daughter, Anna, also went to India in 1822. She was drawn there by her brother's pleading so effectually the cause of the native Indian girls. Dr. Carey's youngest son, Jonathan, a Calcutta solicitor, fell in love with Anna Pearce and they were married in 1824. Carey was highly delighted that his son should be united to the daughter of one he had loved most devotedly. Their home became indeed a Bethany.

And so, we leave this *Brainerd of the Baptists* until we meet him again among the saints of God who have "followed the Lamb whithersoever he went."

John Smith

THE MAN WITH CALLOUSED KNEES

The vivacious, athletic lad stood among a group of rather rough, boisterous companions, enthralling them with his powers of mimicry. How they laughed as he imitated the drawl, or the plaintive tones and gestures of some well-known character who attended the Cudworth prayer meetings! It would have been difficult for an onlooker of such scenes to realize that this same John Smith would one day become the saintly minister who would reap a harvest for Christ.

It was in Yorkshire, England, on January 12th, 1794, that John was born into the home of a lay preacher and his good wife. They had looked forward with joyful anticipation to the birth of their son and surrounded the child with their prayers as they petitioned Heaven for his future usefulness. But it looked for some years as though the Almighty had not heard those requests. When fourteen years of age, it became evident that John was attracted to the more vicious and wicked lads and chose them for his companions. This meant that he soon tired of the restraints of his godly home and decided to immerse himself in worldly activities.

His parents sent him to work with a grocer at Sheffield, but so unsatisfactory was the lad's conduct that he was sent home after two years. Another position was procured for him at Barnsley, Yorkshire, but here, away from the prayers and admonitions of his parents, he gave way to gambling, cursing, and swearing. Being six foot in height and athletic in constitution, he decided to train to be a fighter.

When still only eighteen, however, he heard about a revival at his home at Cudworth. A cousin of his had been converted and, possibly a bit curious, he decided to make a visit and see for himself what was taking place. But he was not prepared for the effect such a brief stay at home would have upon him. Feeling uncomfortable, he decided to leave as quickly as possible. "John," said his mother, "you are wandering about in search of happiness, but you will never find it until you turn to God."[1] Her parting words stung him to the quick.

Turning abruptly, he left her, but found himself trembling and almost ready to cry aloud. Joining his companions on the road, he hurried onward in order to put a distance between himself and the scene of revival. But one could have cut with a knife the atmosphere of silence which encircled the formerly noisy group. Suddenly John cried out, "I am resolved to lead a new life."[2]

Retracing his footsteps, he returned to Cudworth and made his way to the little chapel where the service was in progress. He now knew he was a vile sinner, and so he knelt to pray with Christians who surrounded him until it was time to close the service. A few caring souls who knew how to lay hold on God followed him to his home where they continued in prayer for the lad's salvation. Before morning, John Smith knew he was a child of God and peace reigned in his heart. The father, who had been out on an appointment, returned home to find that his son, so long prayed for, had been redeemed from a life of sin. The burden of years suddenly rolled off his shoulders as he realized that his son had passed from death unto life.

The new babe in Christ now gave evidence of spiritual life by an insatiable appetite for the milk of God's Word. The day after he had received his pardon, the former swearing and gambling young man had read thirty chapters from the Bible. He would place the honored Book upon the counter of the shop where he worked and when no customers demanded attention, he would quickly take a drink of that life-giving Word. Having a very retentive memory, he stored in his mind large portions of that Word which were to be such a help to him in his later ministry.

It is not surprising that a young man of such vivacity and charm needed to watch against every form of encroachment of the enemy of his soul, and this he did by frequently retiring to the woods or some secluded spot where he would come once more into contact with the Being Who, though invisible, was very nigh to the hungry-hearted child of God. A very close friend told how "one day, soon after his conversion, being under peculiar temptation, he retired into a cavern, where he continued for a considerable time, till he felt such an overshadowing of the Divine Presence as quite overwhelmed him; and he has been heard to say," adds Mr. Clarkson, "that had he not often had such visits from the Lord, he never should have been able to persevere in the Christian warfare."[3]

John did not forsake his old companions until he had first witnessed to them as to what God had done for him. He reproved their vices, and exhorted them to turn to the Savior Who was ever ready to receive them. As a result, two of his former friends were converted. And now that he had different values, he realized that he had misspent those years when he could have been filling his mind with useful knowledge. So anxious was he to improve his English that he persuaded several of his companions to join him in utilizing their leisure time in acquiring more knowledge.

Leaving his employment at Barnsley, John attended the Leeds Academy where one of his instructors was David Stoner, a good man, and one prepared by the Lord. Known for his godliness, this professor was an influence for righteousness in the college and never ceased to exhort John to begin preaching. In a letter written to his parents about this time, John says: "In a short time the warfare will be over. A few more conflicts, and we shall be in glory. I feel at present truly happy in my God. Tears of gratitude flow from my eyes for His loving-kindness towards me. Pray that God may help me; for I wish to spend and be spent for Him."[4]

In another letter about the same time, he bared his heart:

> My soul is panting after that mind which was in Christ: in consequence, I meet with many oppositions from Satan; but the Lord is present with me, and supports me constantly under every difficulty. Though I believe that in Christ all fullness dwells, I do not sufficiently look to Him for help and salvation. When I am tempted, I am frequently cast down for a short time; my faith diminishes, and I have not that confidence in God as when everything goes on, or seems to go on well with me. But when I come simply to the Lord, make my case known to Him, acknowledge my weakness, plead the merit of the atonement, and believe on His Name, He delivers me from temptation, lifts upon me the light of His countenance, and causes me to rejoice in Him as my salvation. I can come to Him, through Jesus Christ, and call Him my Father. The Spirit itself beareth witness with my spirit that I am a child of God.[5]

John Smith's first attempt at preaching was in a school-room where David Stoner, his adviser and instructor, had preached his first sermon. He spoke on that verse, "There is a friend that sticketh closer than a brother," but before long he became painfully embarrassed. He finally told the audience that he had nothing more to say and sat down in a state of distress. But this seeming failure did not deter him from further efforts.

Meanwhile, some of his Christian friends were pressing upon him the doctrine of "perfect love" and it deeply affected him as is shown in a letter:

> My heart is given to God. I am seeking and longing for all the mind which was in Jesus Christ. Blessed be God, I am encouraged by His gracious promises to persevere in seeking full salvation. I long to experience this purity of heart. For this I pray, read, study, watch, and trust. It is Thy work, blessed God! Let me enjoy it. In your prayers do not forget him who blesses God for such parents and who daily prays for you.[6]

The demands of the itinerant ministry which he undertook made him realize that he needed this profound transformation in his own life when by faith he would apprehend the fullness of the scheme of Redemption in Christ. He understood that the purpose of Christ's coming had been to "destroy the works of the devil." And where were those "works" more entrenched than throughout the entire fiber of his own inner being? The old Adam nature in him was definitely not subject to God nor could it ever be.

Faith was the most logical thing in the world to him. His biographer said of him in this particular: "To the efficacy of faith he set no limits. If a man were as black as a devil and had upon him all the sins that were ever committed, would he but begin to believe, God would save him." He had been heard to say, "That is the way I rise. I will not suffer myself to dwell on my unfaithfulness: if I did, I should despond."

This man had a remarkable understanding about the nature of faith. "It is well to dare to take God at His Word," he tells us, "to venture on the promises as well as we can, notwithstanding all the opposition and difficulties, until it is easy to lay hold of the blessing, to claim it as ours in all its fullness and glory. . . . We cannot believe too much; we cannot believe too soon. We may rest in Christ for the pardon of our past sins, for the destruction of the body of sin, and for God as our portion. . . . We are kept no longer than we are kept by the power of God through faith."

"He was displeased," his biographer adds, "when persons prayed as if God were unwilling to bless; or when they spoke of unbelief as a mere infirmity. He said: 'It is an abomination when men talk as if they were more willing to bless than God. . . . There is no impediment on God's part. . . . He has given us His Son. It is by justifying God that I sting and stimulate myself to contend. . . . The necessity of wrestling arises not from the unwillingness of God, but from ourselves or Satan; God is the same.'"[7]

It was during his nine months of itinerating in York that John Smith received an abiding sense of the all-pervading love of Christ shed abroad in his heart. His prayer life increased tremendously. There was now something indefinable that energized him.

Upon receiving this endowment of the Holy Spirit in His cleansing and empowering grace, his entire style of preaching was altered. He saw the way in which the flesh can exalt itself even in ministry, and so laid aside homiletical niceties in order to give more room for the Holy Spirit to operate through him. To be thought destitute of talents by those he considered as spiritual leaders in the church, was one of the hardest lessons he had to learn in humility and self-denial. This was especially so when he knew he possessed the ability to embellish his preaching with words of man's wisdom, but he was determined that his preaching would not be with enticing words of man's wisdom but in demonstration of the Spirit Who would never give His glory to man.

This earnest, young Christian would now urge his listeners to expect little by way of progress in the Christian life until the depravity of the human heart were purged. Writing to his parents he says, "The depravity of the heart renders us incapable of doing God's will: it is a disease; it is debility; it pervades the system. But there is 'balm in Gilead,' there is 'a Physician there.'"

John now saw the need of God's direction in the meanest affairs of life. It is easier to consult flesh and blood than to wait upon God for the all-clear before embarking upon any enterprise. A friend of his remarked, "I remember his noticing some step which he had taken, in itself right, but in which he had not first of all ascertained the will of God, as the chief error of his religious life, the effect of which he traced through his subsequent experience."

In the study of biography, it is remarkable to notice how the paths of eminently godly men cross the lives of those who are intent on hungering for more of God. As we have seen, David Stoner helped John as a very young Christian in formulating right principles. Now it was John Nelson who was used of the Lord to further help him. Upon first meeting this distinguished and successful minister, however, the young man had not been too favorably impressed. The godly are often priceless gems hidden in the soil of the field of this world. They need discovery and are generally only recognized by those of like spirit. Knowing the value of lowliness of mind, and meekness of spirit, they do not seek to impress, but are often glad to remain little and unknown. Sitting under Mr. Nelson's ministry, John became convinced of the ever-recurring need of that life-quickening Spirit of God. He writes:

> I have heard Mr. Nelson preach some such sermons as I never heard before. I never saw my littleness as a preacher under any man as much as under Mr. Nelson. He has the unction; this makes him great. He tells me that I must bless God for barren times.
>
> I drag my cold and hard heart to Mount Calvary: if the bleeding Lamb cannot warm and melt it, nothing can. I want more of the dying love of Christ shed abroad in my heart. Lord, help me!

His biographer tells us how important John Smith felt it to be that one should see the depths of man's heart:

> The depravity of the human heart as pictured by Jesus and the Word of God became his study. But who can know the deeps of what is within men? He who preaches to secure the cure must know the malady of sin, and this John Smith determined should be his aim and ambition. . . .
>
> No man feels the value of the soul of another, who has not been made sensible of the worth of his own soul. No man discerns the malignity of sin in the world, who has not felt its bitterness and terror in his own heart. No man is awake to the peril of the ungodly, who has not trembled under the sense of personal danger. No man forms a correct estimate of the value of the atonement, who has not had the blood of Christ sprinkled on his own conscience. In proportion as religion becomes a matter of deep personal interest, will be the concern which a man feels for the salvation of others.

Many of those who have professed this experience of sanctification grow smug and self-satisfied, not living in that moment-by-moment dependence upon God. Not so John Smith! He realized that this demanded a deep and abiding prayer life where one immerses oneself in the Bible, letting God speak through His own Word. In fact, there is no righteousness apart from that which is drawn daily at the Throne of Grace by faith. About this John Smith wrote in a letter:

> There is no substitute for intercourse with God. Without Divine communications, the soul droops and dies and becomes a corrupt thing. But with what life, and beauty, and blessedness God can impregnate the soul![8]
>
> I see there is nothing like entering into God's design concerning us. He wishes to make us perfectly holy and to fill us with all His fullness. We should aim at this; not merely to get to Heaven, but to be as fit for Heaven as we can be,

and to have as much of Heaven as we can have while in this world. In order to this, we must believe much. Let us give credit to God's Word, and realize the blessing in the promise. . . . Let us plead the blood!

O what humblings I have had of late! My soul has been in the dust before the Lord, and at the same time I have felt the confidence of a little child. I love to be in this state. . . . In your class, press the necessity of purity of heart; show that it is received and retained by faith; show it to be a privilege. O, what a happiness to be delivered from all anger, peevishness, pride, malice, and to be filled with gentleness, patience, humility. . . . Let us feast ourselves on Jesus. Let us contemplate Him, our infant Savior, in Bethlehem, and be humbled. Let us listen to Him.

Through his friendship with John Nelson, John Smith had become attracted to his niece, Miss Hamer. A letter to her at this time will reveal what was foremost in his mind:

Let us look attentively into our hearts, look into the written Word, and look up to God for the light of the Spirit to shine upon the heart and the Word. Whatever we discern in us contrary to the Word, let us bring it before the Lord (for we cannot take it away ourselves) and plead with Him until we feel power to venture on Jesus for its destruction. When God speaks to the inmost soul, "Be clean," all corruption and defilement shall depart, and purity shall be diffused through the soul.

Let us not be discouraged, however frightful our hearts may appear, and however feeble and helpless we may feel: Jesus' blood is all-cleansing; Jesus' grace is all-powerful. Jesus is ours by faith. God offers Him to us. O let us lay hold of a whole Savior! Let us force ourselves to the foot of the cross, lift up our eyes, and look to Jesus, till our hearts are pierced to the very bottom with His dying love. "Be ye perfect, even as your Father which is in heaven is perfect." "Be ye holy for I am holy." "For this purpose was the Son of

God manifested" in the flesh, that He might do what? "that he might destroy the works of the devil." O, then, let us say as God says, "Destruction⁻ complete destruction⁻ to sin." Faith, which is a continual and conscious act, will preserve us pure. Let us cry day and night to God for this faith⁻ perfect faith. We shall meet with much opposition. The world cannot do with this; the devil hates this: but few professors will do with this: but the will of God! the will of God![9]

Many decry an experience of this kind lest it unduly exalt the individual. A diary record shows what a low estimate John Smith had of himself:

> I have not had that lively sense of the presence and favor of God the whole of this day, which I wish to enjoy. I am deeply sensible of my ignorance, and of my want of ability for the work of the ministry. Yet the Lord is all-sufficient, and He will qualify and help. I trust I shall be more diligent than I have been. I have to lament my instability in everything. I have not prayed against it as I ought to have done. By the grace of God, I will make a renewed effort.

Ill health, however, soon began to dog the young preacher's footsteps. The symptoms of a malady which was to prematurely end his life began to make their appearance. Writing to his parents he confides:

> I have not been very well. I have had a very bad cough; it has disqualified me, in a great measure, for reading and study. This has made me uneasy: I have spent some almost sleepless nights. I have thought, if God had called me to preach, He would have blessed me with better bodily health. But, blessed be God, I have been much encouraged with seeing and hearing that the Lord condescends to work by me. If the Lord pleases to use me, He has a right to me. He shall have all: body, soul, time, talents⁻ ALL!

Later he wrote to Miss Hamer, now his fiancée: "Get deeper baptisms, signal revelations of the love of God in your heart. Experience the Word; feel that you have the same Spirit that inspired the sacred penmen. Of late, I have had peculiar and severe temptations; and blessed be God, I have had strong and peculiar consolation and support."

John eventually married Miss Hamer and moved to the Nottinghamshire area where he enjoyed revival scenes. Richard Treffey, his biographer, gives an insight into the preparations of soul which preceded that movement of God:

> Shortly after his arrival in the circuit, a pious friend remarked to him one morning that he looked very unwell. He said in reply that he had spent the whole preceding day and night in fasting and prayer, and that he was assured that God would shortly begin a glorious revival in Nottingham and its neighborhood.
>
> Sometime afterwards a few friends called at his house one evening, and found him in a state of deep depression of mind. He had been meditating on the condition of the sinners in the town, and its vicinity, and lamenting with many tears their dishonor of God and His laws. He invited his friends to join him in prayer. One or two engaged in this exercise, and then Mr. Smith poured forth his sorrows before the Lord, confessing and bewailing the sins of the people with great minuteness and indescribable emotion. His vehement agony was so extraordinary that Mrs. Smith, accustomed as she was to witness his exertions, was at length unable any longer to endure the sight and left the room. His friends rose from their knees, and gazed on him with astonishment mingled with apprehension. One of these ventured to expostulate with him, and besought him to cease. Mr. Smith turned to him, and in a tone of inconsolable grief exclaimed, "Go, man, kneel down, and cry day and night for the abominations of the people."

For nearly two hours did he continue to call on God with his utmost strength of body and of mind, and it was by sheer exhaustion alone that he was at last induced to desist. Those extraordinary exercises were accompanied and followed by signs of a coming revival, and in a short time "there was a great rain."[10]

Treffey admits that he had been formerly prejudiced by the reports he had heard of this singular man, but when he had come to Nottingham, he had the privilege of personally scrutinizing him. He had only spent five minutes in his company, however, before he was ashamed of his prejudices and bias. He tells us:

I soon discovered the infinite spiritual disparity which existed between us, but his religion was of an order which conveyed no sort of discouragement to those who contemplated it. It was neither mystical on the one hand, nor exclusive and repelling on the other. There was about it no spiritual empiricism, if I may so express myself. No one who perceived (what it was all but impossible to overlook) the power of his faith, could for a moment hesitate to admit that it was perfectly adequate to the production of his maturity in Christianity. . . .

It was at once perceived that to the simplicity of his faith no spiritual blessing was difficult or remote; and no one could discern the nature of that faith, without being convinced that it was, in its gradations, readily attainable by every sincere and childlike spirit. And this I cannot but consider a principal cause of Mr. Smith's success as a preacher. . . .

He himself sought out the most perfect models of Christian experience, with the rejoicing consciousness that what one believer has succeeded in obtaining was equally within his reach. "When I read Fletcher's life," said he, "I saw a narrow way: not that I had not chosen a narrow way, but I saw one still narrower."[11]

When listening to some friends in a love-feast tell of trials which had driven them to their knees, John commended the action but advised, "There is a more excellent way: that state of mind is to be attained, in which a man shall not need to be whipped to his knees, but shall go to his duty, attracted by the delight which he feels in it."[12]

His humility was most striking. When he had been so ill that his life had been despaired of, he had advised that if he should die, they should place upon his coffin these words, "Unfaithful John Smith."[13]

It would be naturally concluded that a man of such a prayer life and with so serious a concern for others would have little of real humor in his nature. But the Holy Spirit alone can give a balance which man is not capable of attaining by himself. In the following comments on Mr. Smith's character, Treffey gives us a further glimpse of this remarkable man:

> His good nature was unbounded, and in his conversations there was often a quiet, and harmless, but shrewd humor, which gave to his remarks on human nature an unusual vivacity. . . . Mr. Smith seldom refused an invitation to a tea-party, or any social meeting of a similar kind. He was of the same opinion of a great man that "parlor preaching" is a very important part of the duty of a minister. . . .
>
> In addition to those features of his piety which have already been noticed, there were two others which particularly struck me. The first was his luminous insight into the invisible world. On this subject it is not for me to dilate; the veil is on my heart; nor are there many Christians who are capable of estimating this part of Mr. Smith's character. I take this opportunity of confirming the remark of one of his friends, "that he was able to judge of the state of those for and with whom he interceded, by an influence perceptible to his own mind." He had also a peculiar sense of the agency of the

powers of darkness, and of the resistance they offered to the exertion of faith, and the consequent salvation of men. Sometimes this was so impressive, that he actually addressed them as if visibly present, and, in a tone of solemn and mysterious but unwavering confidence, defied their utmost efforts. He once, in private conversation, expressed it as his fixed conviction that their motions were periodical.[14]

John Smith had an intense love for knowledge. His large library contained books both on theology and general literature and he loaned these literary treasures to those of the humblest ranks so that they too might be edified.

Let us observe, however, the grand secret of this man's ability to reach the inmost souls of others. It was none other than prayer⁻ much prayer in secret. He also took the Word of God as his guiding principle. His biographers and friends draw back the curtain of his inmost sanctuary and permit us to see some of his almost unbelievable prayer habits:

> After the family worship of the morning, which Mr. Smith usually prefaced by several hours of private devotions, he returned to the exercises of the closet, and sometimes on his knees and often on his face, wrestled with God, till not infrequently a considerable part of the floor of his study was wet with his tears. In his unreserved disclosures of feeling to his friend, Mr. Clarkson, he once remarked that he was sometimes engaged in prayer for two or three hours, before he enjoyed that unrestricted intercourse with Heaven, which he always desired, and which he generally succeeded in obtaining.
>
> "Often," says another of his friends, "when I have gone to his house with those who were seeking salvation, I have interrupted his devotions, in which he would be so engaged for seven or eight hours at a time." He occasionally spent the

whole night in prayer; sometimes the greater part, if not the whole, of several successive nights: and when he has been from home, the members of the families by whom he had been entertained have, at various hours of the night, been awakened by his groans, when his desires became too big for utterance and his emotions too mighty to be controlled.

Few men have partaken so deeply of that passion which must have been in the heart of our Savior when He prayed for the whole world, and which doubtless motivates Him as He, at this moment, intercedes for His saints. Once, when doctors had advised this prayer warrior to desist from public speaking, he went away to recuperate. When at John Nelson's, he heard of a service in progress and feeling somewhat better, he begged to be permitted to speak for a short time. But again the passionate love for souls poured through his wearied frame, causing him, imprudently, to speak longer than he should have. He hemorrhaged, and it was thought that this untimely effort hastened the end which was not far off.

His last appointment was in Lincoln, but consumption of the lungs was so far advanced that much of his time was spent endeavoring to improve his all-too-small store of strength. He was at last induced to spend some time with his own people. Had he had more oversight, his life might have been extended, but his wife had been unable to go with him to Cudworth. He himself also acknowledged that had he stopped work three months sooner, he might have recovered.

Strong were the attacks of Satan against this soul, but the wounded soldier of the cross would testify to this malignant being that he was redeemed by Christ. He overcame his accuser through the blood of the Lamb. "I have had a mighty conflict with the powers of darkness," he told his father, "but, praise be the Lord, He has delivered me. I have come off 'more than conqueror,' through the blood of the Lamb."[15]

Now greatly enfeebled by the advancing disease, Mr. Smith could scarcely write without much effort. This six-foot tall warrior, once so robust and athletic, was worn out from his incessant labors. He was only thirty-seven when the end came quietly. Those watching with him needed not the rapports of joy in their dying brother to assure them of his triumphant prospects. His entire life had been the witness of his acceptance. After a few mental conflicts he triumphed, saying: "All is clear. I have had some success in my labors, but my happiness does not result from that, but from this: I have now hold of God. I am a very great sinner, and am saved by the wonderful love of God in Jesus Christ. I throw my person and my labors at His feet."[16]

A visitor at his bedside exclaimed, "Glory be to God!" and the dying saint responded "Amen," and then his voice was forever silenced on earth that it might join with the ransomed above in worshiping the Lamb.

Too great a divine voltage of infinite love for souls had poured itself through this limited human channel. It could have had no other effect than to burn it out prematurely. And this was the price John Smith paid for the daily inflow of that God-originated current of compassion for lost humanity. Did he act unwisely? We have no answer to that question. But to save one's life in order to reach the normal span of years and yet have no inflow of such love is a wastage much greater than this seemingly rash expenditure of energy. There is no sadder picture than to see vast stores of human potential expended on mere trifles. Man was made to commune with God and to fulfill his role in the God-determined destiny of the world.

And so we leave John Smith. His labors are over. His victory is certain, and his influence through his diaries, letters, and spiritual children will be finally summed up at the great day of reckoning when each believer shall be awarded according to his deeds.

May John Smith's life inspire each one of us to breathe the following prayer:

"O give me, Lord, that interceding heart
That agonizes vitally for those
Held captive in the sin-producing throes of devilry.
O, let me feel the smart
Of those who learn the intercessor's art
And dare successfully to interpose
'Twixt God and man and take the sinner's part.
Like Moses, sympathetic with the woes
Of sinful Israel, let me intercede with Thee,
O Holy Father, face to face!
And, following the Savior, let me bleed
And suffer for a sin-benighted race;
Prepared like Paul to barter every prize
To bring a sinful people to the skies."

— *D. A. Simons.*

Ann Cutler

Too Young To Die

Ann Cutler was born in Preston, England, in 1759. There is little to know about this striking young woman, so careless of life and so careful for God's kingdom that she had only a brief thirty-five years of life. We do know, however, that she was used of God in bringing about revivals in the mining and weaving areas of Northern England. William Bramwell had been mightily used of God in those parts, and she was counted among his many converts. This eminent minister spent long hours of intercession before he would engage in public ministry and these efforts bore fruit in his converts. Like her spiritual father, Ann Cutler spent many hours in intercessory prayer.

Mr. Bramwell published an account of her useful life, but it has not been our privilege to find a copy. We did come across, however, his brief account of her remarkable labors as quoted by Abel Stevens in his *History of Methodism,* which we share with our readers in the following paragraphs:

> She came to see us at Dewsbury where religion had been and was then in a low state. In this circuit, numbers had been destroyed through divisions. Ann Cutler joined us in continual prayer to God for a revival of His work. Several, who were the most prejudiced, were suddenly struck, and in agonies groaned for deliverance.
>
> The work continued almost in every meeting, and sixty persons in and about Dewsbury received sanctification, and walked in that liberty. Our love-feasts began to be crowded,

and people from all the neighboring circuits visited us. Great numbers found pardon and some perfect love.

The work in a few weeks broke out at Greetland. Ann Cutler went over to Birstal, and was there equally blessed in her labors. She went into the Leeds circuit, and, though vital religion had been very low, the Lord made use of her at the beginning of a revival, and the work spread nearly through the circuit. Very often ten, or twenty, or more were saved in one meeting. She and a few more were equally blessed in some parts of the Bradford and Otley circuits. Wherever she went there was an amazing power of God attending her prayers. This was a very great trial to many of us; to see the Lord make use of such simple means, and our usefulness comparatively but small.

Ann Cutler seemed out of this world, but rather a pure being descended from Heaven to bless the Church in these days of strife. She consecrated herself to a single life, that she might have convenience for public usefulness. "I am Thine, blessed Jesus," she wrote in a formal covenant. "I am wholly Thine! I will have none but Thee. Preserve Thou my soul and body pure in Thy sight. Give me strength to shun every appearance of evil. In my looks keep me pure, in my words pure, a chaste virgin to Christ for ever. I promise Thee, upon my bended knees, that if Thou wilt be mine I will be Thine, and cleave to none other in this world. Amen."

The sanctity and usefulness of her life would have recommended her, had she been a Papal nun, to the honors of canonization. Her piety rose to a fervid and refined mysticism, but was marred by no serious eccentricity of opinion or conduct. It expressed itself in language remarkable for its transparent and pertinent significance and self-possessed demeanor which was characterized by a sort of passive tenderness and a Divine and tranquil ardor. The example, conversation, and correspondence of Wesley, Perronet, and Fletcher, had raised up a large circle of such consecrated women, and had left with them a fragrant spirit of holiness, which was like ointment poured forth about the altars of Methodism.

Ann Cutler seldom addressed the people in public; her power was in her prayers, which melted the most hardened assemblies. She was "instant in prayer." It was her habit to rise, like the Psalmist, at midnight to call upon God; and the time from her regular morning hour of waking, four o'clock till five, she spent in "pleading for herself, the society, the preachers, and the whole Church."

She died in 1794 as she had lived. On the morning of her departure she began, before the dawn, to ascribe glory to the ever-blessed Trinity, and continued saying, "Glory be to the Father, glory be to the Son, and glory be to the Holy Ghost," for a considerable time. At last, looking at her attendants, she exclaimed, "I am going to die. Glory be to God and the Lamb forever!" These were her last words.

Uncle John Vassar

God's Sheep Dog

There was once an artist who had been hired to paint a picture on a building at some height. A scaffold had been erected in order that he might properly execute the job. So enthralled had he become with his masterpiece that he decided to step back and view what the effect would be at a distance, forgetting that he was painting on so narrow a platform. A friend who stood nearby, foreseeing the tragedy about to occur, quickly took up a can filled with paint and threw it over the picture. Aroused and incensed, the artist ran forward to protect his work, thus saving his own life in the process.

Often God must needs allow some tragic circumstance to be thrown across the path of a person who has loved Him, when He sees they have become so absorbed in some plan, project, or earthly Eden that they are missing His best. "I had been ruined had I not been ruined," said a famous man. And many a Christian when he reaches his final goal, will thank God for the upset of plans which terminated his career. He will see the purpose in that frustration or scandal which suddenly spoiled the picture he had been painting. It may even have involved his work for Christ, yet it was making him forget the ultimate end for which his Master had called him.

John Vassar experienced just such a Divine intervention. His family seemed such a complete unit: husband, wife, and two sons. Then in a matter of a few years all but the father were taken. The younger boy sickened and died in September, 1847. The older son of nine years, who was uncommonly gifted, "passed into life" the following autumn after an illness lasting but a few hours. The shock of these two deaths was too much for the wife who, never robust, wasted away, and after a year of suffering joined her two boys in a better Land. John's biographer, Thomas Vassar, writes of this period:

> That cheerless autumn night was the only time we ever saw Uncle John even momentarily cast down. Then for half an hour he did lie down and weep like a heart-broken child. Nor was it strange. Long watching had nearly worn him out. Only four weeks previously, he had closed his venerable father's eyes for the last long sleep. The loves of earth had been breaking fast. But faith quickly rose again and rejoiced in God. The eagle flies highest not in serene but stormy skies, and the believer beats heavenward when the hours are dark and the tempest wild. The heart of the lonely man recovered soon the old peace and trust and exulted in the Rock of his salvation. . . . For those who had gone it was rest and peace. For the one left it was work yet for a little while. . . . He was to be a son of consolation to many a mourner in coming days. He was to minister to smitten spirits with a woman's tenderness. He was to look into eyes dim with tears and say, "I have been in this very pass, and know its bitterness and blessedness."[1]

With every earthly tie broken, Uncle John Vassar felt called to the road, and joining the American Tract Society, he became a colporteur. This gave him access to homes all over the country. And taking up his pilgrim staff, he went forth to round up many a stray sheep. Speaking of himself he said, "I'm nothing but an old shepherd-dog, and I try to help the pastors in tending their flocks."

But let us for a moment acquaint ourselves with John Vassar's early beginnings. His forebears had come of good, old Huguenot stock and had left France because they desired religious freedom and so had come to live in Norfolk, England.

For three generations the Vassars remained there, and then Thomas and his younger brother, James, sailed for America on the ship, Criterion, in 1796. Eventually they settled in Poughkeepsie on the Hudson. Here for a time they engaged in farming, but soon branched out in other kinds of business. Thomas Vassar married Joanna Ellison, twenty years his junior, and to them was born on January 13, 1813, John Ellison Vassar.

John Vassar grew up into an industrious boy and later worked for his father in his brickyards. As a young man, however, he was irreligious, given to blasphemy and possessing a violent, fiery temper. When he was twenty-five, he married a young woman of godly parentage but who, like himself, was irreligious. Now it was that he changed his position and went to work with his cousin, Matthew, who owned a brewery. Diligent in business, he gave promise of becoming, some day, a partner in the firm. And so it seemed that all was going well for John Vassar. His home life was pleasing, his health perfect, and his financial prospects bright.

About this time a revival was going on in Poughkeepsie in the Baptist church and his cousin, Matthew, invited him to attend. John vehemently declined, but at last was hired to go at least one evening. He needed little persuasion to attend a second time, and in this service deep, soul-searching conviction came upon him. He was ashamed of his uncontrollable temper and was deeply convicted for this. That night he could not understand how his wife could sleep when he was on his way to hell so he woke her to tell her so.

So profound was his repentance that it resulted in a born-again experience as clear as that of St. Paul on the Damascus road. He was twenty-eight years of age when this momentous change transpired in his life. And what a transformation! The Bible was placed in a position at work where he could glance at it and meditate on it. Indeed, he showed little tendency to be ashamed of his Lord for he wished to talk to Father even when kneeling among the barrels. "Heaven seemed too far away," he said speaking of his position in the brewery, "when I looked up to it from among the beer barrels."[2] In fact, he soon left the brewery business and, for a time, took up the cause of temperance. As a result, he experienced great opposition in his own home town.

Then it was that tragedy struck. And yet how much poorer the world might have been if the sudden decimation of John's family had not occurred, thus directing him towards a new venture for Christ. It was, after all, his unique adventures in colportage work which made him so outstanding. His consecration was so complete that he was ready to "follow the Lamb whithersoever he went." The love of Christ flowed through him and his dedication to his calling made him ever available so that he was often led of the Spirit to prepared souls. Listening to the Lord of the harvest, he was given intimations of where individuals were who were already ripe to harvest.

His first witnessing was in his own Jerusalem. But Poughkeepsie did not honor its own prophet any more than Jerusalem had recognized Christ as the Messiah. So this ambassador for Christ wended his way westward. Whether it was on foot or in a wagon, this indefatigable sheep dog was ready to follow a stray sheep until he had rounded it up and taken it back to the fold. The illustration of his characteristic faithfulness related below in his own words might help us to understand why this humble colporteur was so mightily used of God:

There was a man in ___ county, a Mr. R___, who lived away from everybody in a log house. I never shall forget the time I had with him. Oh, how he did hate to repent! But he had to at last. Grace was too much for him. And then he had an excellent Christian wife, as so many men have. That helped a good deal. He was fond of his wife, and sometimes he overheard her praying. He knew how she felt about it. I suppose I saw that man twenty times. Sometimes he was good-natured and sometimes he was not.

How mad he would be once in a while, just because I said a friendly word to him about his soul! You see, he was not at ease in his sins. Men never are. They try to be and pretend to be, but they are not. They cannot be. The impenitent sinner is not happy. This man used to be very angry sometimes. But he never struck me. He came pretty near it once or twice. . . . It was after I had known him a good while, that one day when I had gone out into the lot where he was at work to find him, he dropped his hoe and came at me fierce as a lion, cursing and swearing.

I stood still, and he stopped, and we stood and looked at each other. Finally I said, "O, Mr. R___, you will never have any peace till you give your heart to God!" I know that I spoke kindly, for I felt just like crying, I was so sorry for him. But it seemed to make him only angrier still. He fairly foamed at the mouth, and, shouting at the top of his voice, he told me to leave and never let him see my face again, or he would kill me. I did not answer a word, and walked quietly away; but I felt pretty sure that the end was near, and that he could not hold out much longer.

The next time I came that way, as I approached his house, I thought I saw him slip around the corner of the house and make for the barn, like a person trying to get out of sight. I went to the door and asked his wife where he was.

"Oh, my poor husband!" she said, and the tears came into her eyes.

"Have courage," I said; "I believe the Lord will find him this day. Where is he?"

"He told me not to tell you where he was," she replied. "He saw you coming and went out to get away from you, but⁻ but⁻ I think went toward the barn."

"Now, dear sister," said I, "you stay here and pray, and I will go and try to find him." I went out to the barn. I knew that his proud heart must be giving way, else he would not have avoided me so.

I tried one of the barn doors. It was fastened. I knocked. No answer. It was as still as the grave inside.

"O, Mr. R___," I cried, "let me in, do let me in! I'm nobody but a poor sinner saved by grace, and the same grace will save you, if you will only let it! Let me in for Christ's sake; please do!" Then I passed around to another door and found that fastened too, and knocked there, and again I begged him to let me in.

At last, when I began to be afraid I must give him up for that time, as I listened, I heard a sigh and a step, then more steps coming toward me. I heard him unlocking the door. I did not know what was going to happen next. The door opened slowly, and there he stood. You needed to look but once to see that the Lord had won the fight. His face was pale but there was no anger in it. He tried to speak but he could not. I went right up to him and took him by the hand, and said, "O my dear Mr. R___, let us kneel down and thank God together"; and so we did.

There were a good many more tears in that prayer than words, "Now," said he, as soon as he could control his voice, "let us go in and see my wife." I tell you the two minutes it took us to go from the barn to the house were the happiest two minutes he had ever seen. And you ought to have seen that woman's face when she saw us coming in together! She knew what it meant. Besides, a single glance at him was enough. It seems to me I never saw so happy a woman in my life.[3]

Another incident will show how available and obedient to the call of the Master was this faithful sheep dog:

One day, while walking from Poughkeepsie to Pleasant Valley, he overtook a man driving an ox-team along the road. Walking on together in conversation, it was but a minute or two before the Name that is above every name was on the lips of Uncle John, and the subject ever uppermost was broached. With the utmost frankness, and with a trembling voice, the man declared that for weeks he had been secretly trying to grope his way to God. He had said nothing to any one, and no one had said anything to him. All was uncertainty with him and gloom.

That Savior Who "must needs go through Samaria" so long ago, because there was a lost soul waiting to hear words of Life, sent the right man to this inquiring soul that day. Uncle John knew how to meet a case like that. His words fitted that penitent's wants as the notch in the arrow is fitted by the string of the archer's bow. . . . By the roadside they knelt in prayer together, and then they parted, this convert like one in the olden time, going on his way rejoicing.

Hardly had they separated before Uncle John saw a man plowing in a field some distance from the highway. All aglow with the recent interview the question started, "May I not find yonder another such case? Who knows?" Across the lot he hurried, and strange as it may seem, he did find another soul anxious and ready to accept of Christ. In the freshly turned furrows the two knelt and either then or very soon afterward the peace of God entered this heart too.[4]

It was not only plowmen and humble laborers whom this untiring sheep dog would follow. John Vassar was after souls wherever they were. He would also visit door to door in the wealthier districts of Boston and nicknamed a street in one of those exclusive districts "Dives Street." His friend, Rev. J. Hyatt Smith, relates an incident that occurred on that very street:

One day Brother Vassar, while in Cleveland, came to me and said, "Tomorrow I am going through Dives Street (Euclid Street), and I want you to pray for me." I promised him I would, and requested him to report to me the results of his first day's visit to the houses of wealth on that beautiful avenue. I give a report of his visit to the first house on his journey.

At the door of the stately dwelling he met the lady of the house. "What do you want, sir?" she asked as he approached her.

He replied, "I am a colporteur for the Tract Society and," pointing to his basket of books, "I am selling these."

"We have a library," was her reply.

"I don't doubt it," said Brother Vassar, glancing at the building; "but," he continued, nothing daunted by the rather sharp response of the lady, "the truth is, I am legs for Bunyan, Baxter, Flavel, and others. They are all in the basket there."

The lady, evidently struck with the appearance of the man and the quaintness of his address, asked him into the parlor. Having stormed and carried the house he began an assault upon the castle of the heart.

"I am not only a seller of books, but I am anxious to know if you love Jesus," said John.

"I am a member of the church," the woman replied.

"So am I," said Brother Vassar, "but I fear that God will not take our church records. He counts the names recorded in the Lamb's Book of Life."

The attack was fairly commenced, and the arrows of love flew thick and fast. Heart castle surrendered, and the lady with tears exclaimed, "I know it is not enough to belong to a church. You talk like my dear mother. Yes, I trust I do love Jesus."

"Bless the Lord," said John, "that makes us brother and sister. If you love the Savior, and I see you do, would you not like a season of prayer?"

She replied, "I would be glad to have you pray." They knelt side by side, and John poured out his soul in supplication. At the close of the prayer the lady asked, "What is the price of your books?"

"Which one?" asked Brother Vassar.

"All of them," was her answer. Then calling a servant, she bade him carry them to the library, paid Brother Vassar for them, gave him something for himself, and with tears in her eyes begged him to forgive her manner at the door.

"Don't mention it, my sister," said Brother Vassar, "you know what our blessed Master had to bear."[5]

John Vassar knew that well, for a colporteur is often considered by "respectable" folks as a nuisance and of a class to be disdained. Yet he was not one to be easily offended as is seen in the following incident related in *Covenant Weekly:*

> One woman who heard about this strange man and what he was doing, said, "If he comes to my house, he will get the door slammed in his face." Without knowing that the woman had made such a statement, Mr. Vassar rang her doorbell the next day. When she saw that he was the man who had been described to her, she slammed the door in his face. John Vassar sat down on her doorstep and sang:
>
> > "But drops of grief can ne'er repay
> > The debt of love I owe,
> > Here, Lord, I give myself away;
> > 'Tis all that I can do."
>
> The woman heard the earnest verse as he sang, and was convicted a sinner. She opened the door and called Mr. Vassar in, who led her to Jesus Christ.

"I do not think his character had those stages of growth which mark most Christian men," Rev. Hyatt Smith concludes. "In Christ Jesus he seemed to have been born a man of full stature. It is said of the river Jordan that, unlike most streams, it does not start with small springs and receive the contribution of rivulets by the way, so attaining fullness, but bursts forth from one vast source, a river rolling to the sea."[6]

Five years after his wife's death, John Vassar married again, but before doing so he informed his intended partner that she would face continued sacrifice in that he would be away from home a good share of the time. He was divinely called, and nothing must hinder the Master's complete possession of his life.

The frequent travels of this lowly colporteur often necessitated his being entertained in the homes of ministers. Occupying the pulpit of a prominent Baptist Church in Boston at that time was A. J. Gordon, a very Spirit-filled minister, who gladly welcomed Uncle John Vassar into his home. He came to revere and honor him and gives the following tributes:

> I can truly say that I never received such quickening and inspiration from any other living person. And though I cannot follow his steps, I trace those steps with the most intense admiration. His was a life so given up to God that I believe it would have been literally impossible to have given any more; a communion with God so unbroken that it may be justly said the language of earth, its chatter, its frivolity, was a foreign speech to him, while the language of Heaven was his true "mother tongue."
>
> To one who never met him, it would be quite impossible to describe the impression which he instantly made on meeting him. He gave one a powerful electric shock the moment he touched him. There was such an intensity of zeal, accompanied with such a magnetic manner, that the impression was instantaneous and quite overwhelming. . . .
>
> I recall with deepest interest his singular consecration and prayerfulness. Is it possible for one to live for a single end⁻ the glory of God in the salvation of souls⁻ and to pursue that end with all the ardor and enthusiasm with which the merchant pursues a fortune or the politician an office? It is good to find, in this skeptical age, one life that can answer that question without any qualification.
>
> This man knew nothing else, thought of nothing else, asked for nothing else, but this one thing. When he came occasionally to work among my flock, he at once took the whole church and people on his heart and began to travail for them in prayer, as though his very life depended on the issue. This intercession continued "night and day with tears," as long as he was with us. He never said, indeed, that he had prayed all night. But I could hear him again and again breaking forth in the darkness "with strong crying" unto God, and I knew what the burden was. It was this congregation, strangers to him till today. It was this flock, not one of whom he ever had seen till now. . . .

With a soul knit into unbroken fellowship with Christ, he had become "baptized into a sense of all conditions." He did not love men with the natural heart any longer. He could say with Paul, "God is my record, how greatly I long after you all in the bowels of Jesus Christ." This habitual prayerfulness was something so wonderful that I wish to emphasize it as furnishing the true secret of his life. A lady at whose house he spent a night told me that in the morning her Roman Catholic servant girl came down and, with an astonished expression, said, "Mrs. B___, that old man was praying all night. I could not sleep, it made me feel so. But I should never be afraid with such a man in the house."

What always struck me as most remarkable in his personal conversations was their absolute abruptness. In scores of interviews of the sort which I have witnessed, I never once remember his introducing his subject with any preliminary remarks. He came at once to the theme. His first question, after the ordinary salutation, was generally the vital question, "My friend, will you kindly permit me to ask, have you been born again?"

This method I think he adopted deliberately, as having been proved by years of experience the wisest. Noticing the shock and revulsion which this abrupt approach sometimes produced, I used to regret that he was not more circuitous in his advance. But I confess that with larger experience I have changed my mind and come to the conclusion that the directness is the most vital condition of success in personal conversation. . . .

The results were varied, of course. The person addressed was always stunned and startled, sometimes made angry, but in multitudes of cases wounded into life. There was never the slightest tinge of severity, mark you, in the abruptness. . . . I generally heard from his visits and sometimes in anything but complimentary terms. But he left an impression which could not be shaken off, and from which fruit, in some cases, was gathered years after.

In a very appreciative notice of him by a well-known minister he speaks of the habit of going from house to house with his inevitable question, and says, "I have known him to set the whole town in an uproar by the spiritual census taking. But when his subsoil plowshare had turned the community upside down, then was the time for fruitful work." And that is true. The very offense which he so frequently gave was often the open door into hearts hitherto hopelessly closed.

The life of which I am speaking made a profound impression in another direction, by the startling contrast which it presented to the ordinary quality of piety in the church. I pass, in saying this, from the power of Christian conversation, to that of Christian example. A humble man who never talked of himself, except in terms of depreciation, and to whom any suggestion of credit or praise always seemed painful, he at the same time gave the most powerful illustration which I have ever witnessed of utter and unreserved consecration to God. . . .

We talk admiringly of apostolic zeal and primitive piety, *but let a genuine fragment of this piety suddenly fall into the midst of us, and I am not so certain that it will be greeted with unqualified applause.* Extremes can never meet without commotion. A red-hot enthusiasm for Christ plunged suddenly into an element of lukewarm piety will inevitably produce a hissing and ebullition. Contrariety of character is sufficient to awaken antagonism, even if there is no hostility of spirit. This principle holds everywhere, in doctrine, in life, in morals. The bare, silent presentation of a startling contrast is a signal for disturbance. . . .

Well, he did rouse a commotion wherever he went. And, as the writer whom I have previously quoted says truly, "his most vehement opposition came from the class represented by the elder brother in the parable of the Prodigal Son." The respectable, moderate, prudential churchman, whose chief concern is that the religious proprieties be not jostled, was stunned and confounded by his impetuous zeal. The dweller-at-ease in Zion was indignant at the wanton invasion of his comfort which this "hot Gospeller" brought. . . .

And so would come charges of insanity made to the face⁻ the old clamor, "Thou art beside thyself." The minister who was harboring this disturber often was warned to send him away lest the church might be driven to mutiny. And thus, as he illustrated marvelously one part of Scripture, "The zeal of thine house hath eaten me up," he received the literal fulfillment of the other part, "The reproaches of them that reproached thee are fallen upon me."[7]

In these days of such appeals for money, it is difficult to understand the total disinterestedness of John Vassar. A. J. Gordon again commends this colporteur for his simple trust in God for all his needs:

Instead of being perplexed to acquire money, as so many Christians are, he seemed greatly perplexed, if any came into his hand, to know what to do with it. If a ten-dollar gold piece were slipped into his pocket, as was often done by some grateful convert, he would act like a citizen of Heaven wondering whose "image and superscription" this could be, and what possible value this coin could have for him, "a stranger and a pilgrim on the earth." If I were to describe his peculiarities in this direction, I fear it should make him appear almost grotesque in his indifference to the things of this world.[8]

Before concluding this brief sketch of this unusual man of God, we would like to point out that John Vassar possessed a sensitivity to the leadings of the Holy Spirit to an extraordinary degree. He was ready and available to go anywhere for God. When he had proved the truth of that old proverb, "No prophet is without honor save in his own country," he was ready to go West. And when the Civil War broke out, and the soldier boys needed a kindly, loving man to minister, Uncle John was a welcome figure to those lads who were so uncertain of tomorrow. He would bring in supplies of soap, pencils, pens, paper, and other simple commodities which they needed, and then would give himself to their soul's welfare.

After the war, when John realized that there were few Sunday Schools through parts of the South and few men available to do such work, he readily stepped into the gap. Hundreds of black children hovered around the kindly old man as he ministered to them. Then, when down in Florida, he saw vast areas where there were no preachers in a sixty mile radius. When a minister felt the need of an assistant in a revival effort, Uncle John was again available.

His cousin Matthew Vassar, a wealthy brewer, liberally endowed and built that imposing and noble structure, Vassar College. John Vassar chose the humbler and less prestigious role of a colporteur. But when on December 9, 1878, his funeral was held at Poughkeepsie on a day that was dark with storm, many, in spite of the weather, came to pay their last tribute to the warrior who had braved the storms of life, and had now entered into rest.

"If he had a coat of arms," his pastor, Rev. Kendrick, told the assembled crowd, "the proper device for it would have been a burning heart. Though zealous, he was not censorious. He lived in a higher sphere of spiritual life than his brethren, but he was always most patient with them. 'He allured to Heaven and led the way.' . . . If no opportunities offered for doing good, he went in search of them. In this respect I have never known his like."[9]

> "'Twas a glorious exchange for him!
> His sword laid down, he took the scepter up;
> His call to arms, changed to the victor's song;
> His war-torn banner, to triumphant robes,
> His dying bed, to an undying throne."[10]

George Railton

THE MAN WHO CARED INTENSELY

Two very devout and intensely earnest Christian men were born on the same day, July 6, but some hundreds of years apart. One was John Huss of Bohemia, the other George Railton of the Salvation Army. Both were men who held their convictions very sacredly and were ever conscious of an undying obligation to their generation. Both had very stormy careers: that of Huss ended in martyrdom while Railton's included a prolonged period of thirty years or more of standing quite alone in a movement he dearly loved and with which he remained until his death.

By the time George Railton appeared on the scene, the religious world had so adjusted itself to mediocrity, that when it discovered a man who felt that his food, his clothing, his sleep, and his family were all subordinated to "this one thing I do," it could not help but conclude that, "he was beside himself." Yet Christ's own brethren had at one time said the same thing of Him. And so it is not surprising that those whose love for Christ and His kingdom surmounts every other consideration are counted eccentric or, to put it colloquially, "a bit touched in the head." Older men shook their wise heads over one so young as Railton who believed in "praying until your knees were petrified and preaching until you were too hoarse in order to make yourself heard."[1]

The life story of George Scott Railton is indeed a fascinating one. He was born of missionary parents who were very decided in their ideas of Christian devotedness. It may have been the high quality of Christianity George saw his parents live out before him which caused him to view a bit apprehensively the costliness of being an out-and-out Christian.

At seven years of age, young as he was, George eluded God, perhaps not wishing a confrontation with One so demanding in self-denial and sacrifice. In any case, he managed to live his own life, seemingly safe from Divine interference, until at ten years of age he fell ill with a rather dangerous form of influenza which was taking a toll of even the strong. George had overheard adults talking about this insidious illness. Lying in bed, he began to seriously consider his position with the God with Whom he had been at odds.

He had always argued that, like the dying thief, he would prepare to meet his Maker upon his death bed, but this kind of flu was known to plunge the patient into unconsciousness. The deeply-thinking lad knew that if he left his salvation too late, he might not be able to make a sensible commitment of himself to God. So while his parents were out at a service, George made his solemn pledge to the Lord and was born again. The joy that flooded his soul was such that he danced around the room forgetting his former pain and miserable feelings.

The boy had no question about his acceptance with his Heavenly Father, and he also believed that after the new birth there was an experience of full consecration resulting in heart purity which was available to all. Yielding his life totally to his Maker, George received the blessing of a cleansed heart at the age of fifteen. This experience proved to be genuine as his whole after-life illustrated.

Four or five years later, cholera raged in the area where he lived, and few wished to endanger their lives by contact with the dying. George's parents, however, could not escape the conviction that their duty lay in giving themselves to the stricken. In a short time they both succumbed to the disease, leaving their sons orphans. Launcelot, the older brother by six years, had decided upon the Methodist ministry, but George was only a schoolboy as yet.

The time soon arrived, however, when he had to face the world. It was while working for a relative in the shipping business that his Christian principles were put to the test. George could not consent to write the letters for the company, for he felt the truth was being sacrificed for the sake of prospective sales. So the plucky youngster was dismissed and soon found himself adrift in the vast world.

The printed page is used of God at moments when a soul is at the cross roads and does not know which way to go. A booklet written by William Booth came into the hands of the orphaned youth when he was in his early twenties, and the rousing words of this enthusiast found an echo in George's own heart. He had tried the Methodist Church, but his intensity of feeling about soul-winning found little there to kindle the flame of devotion which was already warming his whole being.

George lost little time in making contact with the Booths. The attraction was mutual. They found in this down-to-business Christian youth just what they were needing at that moment, and the young man discovered in these two warm-hearted, mature Christians an unusual sense of unity of purpose. He was to live in their home for eleven years while he worked as their assistant. He found in Mrs. Booth especially, one whose heart beat as his own on this subject of entire devotedness to God.

Being unusually gifted, George found ample opportunity during those early days of the Army for writing challenging articles in which he could make known the ideals and aims of this group. It was George Railton who contributed to the Salvation Army its military language and its soldier-like attitude. He himself was prepared to live out the barracks' life, demonstrating that there is a warfare in which a Christian must engage if he is to pluck souls from the burning.

This young saint scarcely cared to give a thought about what he put on. Mrs. Booth had to more than once remonstrate with him about his appearance. Sleep and food were mere incidentals compared to the importance of the work in which he had engaged. How he enjoyed the councils of war he had with the General and his young son, Bramwell!

The Booths eventually sent George to pioneer in the United States for the Army. Souls were won as the invader took over city after city. Hardship and toils meant little. But he was not to be there long, for the much-needed recruit was recalled to help at London headquarters. Often he would stay up until the small hours of the morning, working in the office with Bramwell, and then snatching a few hours' sleep on a bench before beginning a new day.

The Salvation Army was at that time receiving harsh treatment from the mobs, and the authorities were unsympathetic with these intruders into the religious life of Britain. Some were imprisoned; others were injured, and yet new soldiers were daily enlisting under the "blood and fire" banner. But none of this moved George. "Deliverance from every thought of self-interest," he once remarked, "and from every particle of fear as to what men can do, which fits people to pass through dark and hard periods unmoved . . . is for everyone who will seek it."

In the meantime, George shocked some of his friends by his marriage to Maryanne Parkyn of Cornwall. They did not judge him to be of the marrying kind. Maryanne was the only daughter of a Free Church minister and a man of property. She, however, had already braved her father's disapproval in becoming a Salvationist and had begun to play the tambourine in open-air evangelism. The two had first met in an all-night of prayer at London, and George had escorted Maryanne to her home after the service. Right from the beginning, they discovered they had much in common, and before long were married, engaging together in the work of the Mission, and it is not surprising that Maryanne proved in every way to be a proper helpmeet for her rugged husband.

At first, there had been opposition on the part of her father who objected to her marriage with a Salvationist, but an interview of one hour with Railton convinced him of the man's integrity. Others felt the same. A friend, an old scientist, asked Maryanne to visit him and astonished her with the question, "What have you ever done that you should marry such a man?" Then looking at her sternly, he continued, "Let me tell you, that man is absolutely unique. I am not religious, and I study men from a psychological point of view only. I went to see the Salvation Army and I found a man for whom I have a profound admiration, and whom I consider as one in a generation. Well, come into my study and I will give you some hints."[2] Unfortunately, not all of her friends were of the same opinion.

On her honeymoon, the young wife was to have her first encounter with George's intense love for the souls of others. She had thought these ten days would be a relaxation for the man she loved, but instead, they were filled up with working for the salvation of those who came to visit them. She discovered too, how little he cared about their first dwelling place, leaving it to others to choose for them. Maryanne was at first shocked and wondered what her friends would think of her humble abode. But that was not all. She was soon to discover that her husband would never spend a Christmas at home, for he wished to follow in the footsteps of Him Who left His Father's home to spend Christmas with those He came to save.

In spite of the many separations and untold hardships Maryanne experienced as the wife of a Salvation Army Commissioner, she could still say after thirty years of married life: "An extraordinary affection came into our hearts. I almost worshiped him. I never thought that any human being could be like him. I know no two people who were nearer to each other than we." The one thing that bothered her about her husband was that, as she herself puts it, "He was absolutely determined to kill himself with over-work."[3] It seems pretty certain, however, that as the years passed, Maryanne came to share her husband's belief that: *"The more we follow Christ, the better we shall get on and the worse we shall be despised and hated."*[4]

The above statement was written in a letter to Colonel Clibborn who was to later marry one of General Booth's daughters. Afraid that the young Colonel was in danger of catering too much to public opinion in order to gain publicity, he continues: "I'm certain the Army is being crushed by the perpetual series of meetings to extol it to the skies, and I dread the effect of these reports showing the introduction of these genteel horrors of magistrates and celebrities to our platform."[5]

In a letter to the Booths he writes:

> The simple truth is, *we cannot gain the apostolic results we desire without the apostolic price.* We are paying the price in full, I firmly believe, and if so, God cannot fail to supply all our need. He satisfied me yesterday that no matter what floods of anguish and shame we might have to go through, He would keep us up, and give us according to our faith after it all. It is not according to our strength or our wisdom or our ability, or even our efforts, but according to our faith.[6]

For himself, he viewed the life of a soul-winner with all its denials and hardships in a light vein. Writing in the autograph book of a young person, he said: "The life of a soul-saver is the grandest, merriest, strangest life that can be lived on earth⁻ the life of Jesus lived over again in us. It will cost you all, but it will be a good bargain at that!"[7]

When Mrs. Booth died of cancer in 1890, Bramwell became his father's assistant. As time went on, George Railton saw with dismay certain tendencies beginning to creep into his beloved Army that smacked to him of the flesh rather than of the Spirit. The first departure he noticed was the business ventures in which the General and his son were engaged. Another was that the rich and politically influential were being asked to appear on their platforms. But the most distasteful of all to Railton was the Army's involvement in the insurance business.

At a World Congress of the Salvation Army, when many of her soldiers gathered from all over the world, George Railton appeared barefooted and in sackcloth. The audience only smiled tolerantly as they watched this unusual man take his place on the platform. They knew their zealous compatriot, but they were not prepared for what followed. When testimony time came, Railton stood up and began speaking. The stenographers taking down the messages were too stunned to record his exact words, and so it was that few could remember precisely what he had said. But the gist of it was that the Salvation Army was departing from self-denial and the simplicity of living by faith, thus resorting to fleshly methods. After speaking, the rugged Commissioner held up a paper which was an announcement of the Insurance Scheme. Putting it under his feet, he stamped upon it in disdain.

George Railton sat down. There were a few hearts, doubtless, which beat in unison with his, but there were others who were utterly dismayed. The General and his son Bramwell later endeavored to extort an apology from Railton, but the pilgrim soldier knew he had acted solely out of deep sorrow of heart as he watched the organization he had so dearly loved beginning to major in social work and introducing various forms of compromise with the world.

Was not Israel at one time at the very same place as the Salvation Army? They had had God in the pillar of fire to go before them by night and He had stood so close that He was the cloud by day. He had supplied them with manna, and had known where to command the rock to yield refreshing water in that desert land to quench the thirst of hundreds of thousands. Divinely appointed judges had represented God to Israel for many years, and the Almighty had been enough. Now they desired to imitate the heathen nations round about. Samuel, the prophet, pleaded with them, but to no avail.

God gave them what they wanted: kings in costly array, armies with more sophisticated weapons and with chariots and horse-men! But God warned them through His prophet that their decision would be costly. They had not rejected Samuel but God. Had their Divine Leader not furnished a table in the wilderness? Had He not been the Commander-in-Chief, the Lord of hosts, calling all the forces of nature to assist the wandering, helpless band of Israelites in their warfare against unnumbered foes?

At the time of the reign of Solomon, Israel was at her height as far as luxurious buildings were concerned. Forbidden wives from many heathen nations occupied a prominent place in the king's sumptuous court. Then, too, Solomon indulged in commerce in horses and chariots which trade Moses had forbidden Israel. "Woe to them that go down to Egypt for help; and stay on horses, and trust in chariots," Isaiah wrote as he saw the same evils of which Moses had forewarned. Silver and gold, too, were plentiful, but after Solomon died, the people revolted under the heavy taxation. Outward splendor always makes its demands upon the common people. The kingdom of Israel then started her downward slide, ending in ignominious captivity under Babylon. Where was her purported glory? Her drift had been so gradual that the nation had not recognized the terrible decline until too late. So often the history of a denomination, once existing only by its faith in God, reveals its degeneration until its whole complex pattern is merely an imitation of the church which lost her first love.

Railton did not want his beloved Army to follow this tragic pattern. He doubtless did not grasp to the full extent the financial problems of that growing Army, nor did he have that balance necessary for organizing so vast an organization. But did God wish that group to expand so rapidly? This will not be known until the Great Day. Once when Oswald Chambers thought of praying in a certain manner for a Bible School, he refrained for fear he might be asking for that institution to last longer than the fulfilling of God's purposes required.

George Railton was to suffer long and hard for his outspokenness. He was not martyred as had been many of God's servants, but there are other ways to punish recreant followers. He was given the silent treatment. To be set aside after having entered so fully into the innermost councils of the early Army was a heavy cross. Explanations were made by headquarters which hinted that the ardent soul-winner had overdone in his zeal and was a bit affected in his mind. Father and son were very secretive about the whole affair, and George was warned not to speak to others about his convictions. It is noteworthy that a biography of Railton, written in those earlier days by loyal officers, omitted mentioning his differences with the Booths.

A trip abroad was planned for him and, accompanied by his faithful wife, the overtired, stunned soldier refrained from any activity until he had regained his health. The journal he kept on this voyage was destroyed by order of General Booth. After the voyage, Railton became a roving evangelist, still maintaining an amazing loyalty of heart to the Army and its General. But further misunderstanding came when a son-in-law of the Booths, wishing to do what he could to heal the breach, asked for Railton to write quite openly to him about his convictions. But when the letter was received, it was handed to the General who mistook the motive of the writer as an effort to disunite the family.

No one but those who have suffered in like fashion can know that anguish which results from old wounds being reopened, an experience which must have lacerated the heart of this loyal soldier. Was it disloyalty which caused George Railton to shout warning when the ship he loved so well was heading for the rocks? Was it not rather love which sprang from the highest motives which kept the valiant soldier standing in the way and pleading for a return to the old paths? Charlotte Perkins Stetson has written a poem on this subject that expresses this kind of love:

"It takes great love to stir the human heart
To live beyond the others and apart.
A love that is not shallow, is not small,
Is not for one or two, but for them all.
Love that can wound love for its higher need;
Love that can leave love, though the heart may bleed;
Love that can lose love, family and friend,
Yet steadfastly live, loving, to the end.
A love that asks no answer, that can live
Moved by one burning, deathless force to give.
Love, strength, and courage; courage, strength, and love:
The heroes of all time are built thereof."

The shut door to headquarters opened the door to a world-wide ministry. Was there a lonely outpost with only a few struggling warriors? Railton loved to visit them and give them support. Was it some field as yet unopened by the Salvation Army? Railton was ready to go. Nothing would induce him to be accompanied by an aide, although the Booths kindly offered this. He preferred to travel by the lowest class available, for did not the common people respond more to Jesus when He walked among men?

At twelve noon each day wherever he was, George Railton would kneel in prayer to God, be it on a train, boat, or in the market place. His boys had often been embarrassed when, in front of their school chums, their soldier-father would bend his knee to the King of kings at that noon hour.

Then he also had taken the vow of poverty, like his Leader before him, and he would eat but little and sleep sometimes on a pile of *War Cries*. His wife, deeply concerned about her husband's health while on these journeys abroad, persuaded some officers to see that, when leaving for the next country, he would have at least the price of one meal in his possession. This had to be done stealthily, for George Railton was determined to be true to his desire to be a pilgrim and stranger on earth. Perhaps no traveler in the Lord's service has visited as many countries as did this lone servant of Christ. Japan, China, South America, Germany, France, Switzerland, Denmark, Finland, Norway, Sweden⁻ all became the field of his commission. In summing up those years both of pain and of possibility, Railton might well have echoed the sentiments expressed in the following lines:

> "What if all doors of the world close roughly
>   One by one in the pilgrim's face?
> But for the boon of that rude out-thrusting
>   He had missed the way to his loftiest place."

Meanwhile, the faithful wife who had to remain at home, would have to frequently nurse her husband back to health after break-downs due to strain, overwork, and undue exposure. When at the birth of her children she recognized their physical frailness, she knew that she could not accompany her husband on his long trips. The children grew up not having known much of their sainted father. But whether alone or with the family, his loyalty to Christ remained unsullied: "I have been asking God," he wrote to Maryanne not long after they were married, "to help us always to run after Jesus just as if He were newly manifested."[8]

Though for over thirty years, this untiring soldier of Christ kept a love and loyalty for his General and for the organization, not once would he bow to the pressures to condone the fleshly departure from the simple course adopted in the early years. "Not he that succeeds to the end," he exhorted, "but he that endureth to the end shall be saved. Let all your efforts, your sacrifices, your life itself, be lost to all appearance. God has said you shall reap in due season. Be satisfied."

One might ask the question, "Why did Railton remain within the organization?" The answer lay in his loyalty which was just as diamond-like in quality as was his determination to register his warnings about what he considered to be the Army's departures from Biblical principles. No other group offered him the opportunities for soul-winning which the Salvation Army did. No other leader still could command his respect as the General with whom he had started out.

Railton always felt that he would doubtless die at his post. "Far from expecting to live out much of my second half century," he wrote on one of his birthdays, "I know that I may at any moment pass into the Overcomer's Fatherland. . . . Today's great news to me has been that of Major Elmslie's glorious rush up the railway station steps into Heaven, and I wish for no better ending to my warfare."[9] God indulged His loyal servant by granting his desire as we shall see.

George Scott Railton was sixty-three years of age when he embarked on what proved to be his last earthly journey. He seemed to have a presentiment that this European trip might be his last. Unknown to his wife, he wrote to his two boys saying he would be gone for a long time and they would not see him unless they came then, and yet, according to his plans, he was only to be gone for a few weeks.

After assisting the Peyrons in an evangelistic campaign in Switzerland, where it was noted he seemed to have had a renewal of youthful strength and joy, Commissioner Railton set out for Holland on his return trip home. Having to make a stop-over at Cologne, Germany, he spent the evening at the Salvation Army center there and then made his way to the train station. Realizing he might miss the train if he did not hurry, and carrying his few possessions stuffed in one bag, the lone traveler rushed up the stairs and through the gates to the waiting train which was about to leave. A few moments later, when the ticket collector made his rounds, he noticed Railton's condition with alarm and lifted his body off the train. The nearby Salvation Army hostel was notified and his friends soon arrived at the station to discover that the lonely, misunderstood but true St. George had made his last attack upon Satan's citadel. He had been faithful unto death, and was now beyond the reach of calumny, belittlement, and weariness. The last step had been taken and the goal reached.

In the pocket of his uniform was found a paper giving directions as to what to do in the event of his death and making clear that the Salvation Army was to be notified first as he wished it to be known to the last minute to whom he belonged. The paper was written in Railton's own hand and in three languages ̄ English, German, and French. It read:

Address: 101, Queen Victoria Street,
London, E. C.

If found anywhere dead or unconscious, please if dead, bury on the spot as quickly and cheaply as possible, reporting as above.

If any church close by will bury, good. If not, do not trouble. But report.

If found unconscious: get into any hospital. I do not want to burden anyone.

You can rely on The Salvation Army to pay any really needed costs, as of a poor man⁻ no flowers.

101 (Salvation Army headquarters) will report to my dear wife and family; but I do not want any of them to have the cost and misery of coming to bury or nurse me. My love to everybody. Amen. I am going to Heaven. Meet me there.[10]

His wife and eldest son immediately made their way to Cologne where his body lay, and Maryanne wrote a long account of those days in Germany for the benefit of many interested friends. "We had taken out his last passport," she writes, "and at four o'clock the next morning he began his journey 'home,' with the final permission of the authorities of the Fatherland 'to pass on unhindered and without delay.' But the angels had brought him that permission a few days before, and I think he was already at work in another Land while we said we were 'taking him home.' And so ended his last visit to his beloved Germany."[11]

He was given honors at his funeral, General Bramwell Booth saying: "Railton's affection for me passed that of a brother beloved. My loss and the loss of The Army are great indeed. He was the last legacy left to me by my dear Father, who on his death-bed said in one of our parting talks, 'Railton will be with you.'" And after a brief silence he added three words, "And he was." Later at a Memorial Service, Bramwell Booth said if he were to write his epitaph it would be, "He Believed God."[12]

We conclude this fascinating life-picture of George Scott Railton with a poem he wrote and pray that the example of this

modern saint may inspire others to the same disinterested love
for Christ and His kingdom on earth:

> "No home on earth have I,
>   No nation owns my soul,
> My dwelling place is the Most High,
>   I'm under His control.
> O'er all the earth alike,
>   My Father's grand domain,
> Each land and sea with Him I like,
>   O'er all He yet shall reign.
>
> "No spot on earth I own,
>   No field, no house be mine;
> Myself, my all I still disown,
>   My God, let all be Thine.
> Into Thy gracious hands
>   My life is ever placed;
> To die fulfilling Thy commands,
>   I march with bounding haste.
>
> "With Thee, my God, is home;
>   With Thee is endless joy;
> *With Thee in ceaseless rest I roam;*
>   With Thee, can death destroy?
> With Thee, the east, the west,
>   The north, the south are one;
> The battle's front I love the best,
>   And yet⁻ Thy will be done!"[13]

John G. Govan

THE PIONEER OF RURAL EVANGELISM

The villagers were eagerly awaiting the arrival of the young preacher from nearby Glasgow who was coming to hold a series of Gospel services. As a Scottish gentleman looked out of the window, he exclaimed to his wife with evident disappointment in his voice, "Why, he's only a boy! If this is the evangelist, I am afraid there will be nothing done here." But the following days proved how mistaken he was, for God was with the "boy," and it is interesting to learn how he became a mighty power for God.

John G. Govan, who later became the founder of the Faith Mission, was born on the 19th of January, 1861, into a family of twelve¯ six girls and six boys, five of whom became preachers and writers. His father, William Govan, was a Glasgow businessman and a member of the City Council. During the fierce persecution of the Covenanters two centuries earlier, one of his ancestors had sealed his testimony with his own blood in the Grassmarket, Edinburgh. John's mother, Margaret Arthur, was the English-born daughter of a Congregational minister.

This, then, was the rich inheritance which was passed on to "Donnie," as he was fondly called by his family. In his book, *In The Train of His Triumph,* he tells about his early turning to Christ when twelve years of age:

> I was converted when quite young, through an address
> my father gave on a Sunday evening at Corrie, in Arran, where
> we were staying one summer. That address made a great

impression on me, as a boy of twelve, and I gave my heart to Jesus and trusted Him to forgive me my sins.

But there was not much of Christ about my life, and I do not think I testified to my conversion till several years later. After I left school there was a real heart backsliding, never right into sin, but just to the level of my worldly companions, always feeling at the same time that I was converted, that I trusted Jesus as my Savior, and would go to Heaven when I died.

I began to keep a diary when I first entered business at the age of nineteen. I notice that it is chiefly taken up with reference to games, business affairs, and political interests. I was a Sunday School teacher, and a monitor in a boys' meeting, but this was more a matter of duty than of interest, and the chief talk among the monitors used to be the football match of the day before. . . . This was the condition of heart before the Lord began to wake me up. He set me to Christian work, but at first there was not much joy in it.[1]

At this time, however, many powerful influences entered his life. The whole family faithfully attended the services conducted by the evangelists Moody and Sankey and were greatly blessed. "My father was closely associated with them in the work in Glasgow," John explains, "and I attended about forty of the meetings. These meetings greatly stirred me, and for the first time I began to speak to people about their souls, and to feel my need of spiritual blessing."[2]

His father's death about this time made a profound impression upon him, for, in his farewell message to the family, he had especially stressed that John was to be a witness and bear testimony for Christ.

When the Salvation Army invaded Scotland, one of the lady workers stayed with John's brother who lived next door to him. The fragrance of her life greatly influenced the Govans and it is not difficult to trace at this time the hand of the divine Planner in preparing more than one of this family for service in the great harvest field of the world. Under the preaching of Catherine Booth and others, Jamie Govan, two years older than John, came into a deep experience with God at this time. There was a quality of spiritual life that at first puzzled the younger lad, and then produced deep longings for similar reality. John says:

> He had a joyful religion which I did not understand. In the morning I could hear him singing in his bedroom, and I considered this absurd. Then I did not like people saying, "Hallelujah," and tried to avoid coming into too close contact with such persons. I did not mind earthly happiness, but religious happiness I did not approve of.
>
> One day some person did something very unkind to this brother, something that I would have considered aggravating, and I said down in my heart, "Now we shall see him lose his temper!" But he did not, and I could not understand it. If anything like that had happened to me, I should have been sure to lose my temper.[3]

Jamie had a radiance and a power about him, both appealing and challenging. He would speak about cases of spiritual blessing, as he and John walked the five miles to "Salvation Hall" which he had opened in Pollokshaws to reach the many local factory workers and their families with the Gospel. "Other lords beside thee," the older brother would quote, "have had dominion over us." As he spoke, the words pierced the heart of the younger man, who knew only too well the domination of those "other lords": worldly ambition, pride, fear of man, and many more. In later years John Govan recalled:

> I do praise God for the testimony to holiness in lives lived before me in those days. I began to long for a better experience, and the Lord began to prepare me. I have found that sanctification is nearly always gradual in preparation, though instantaneous in reception. I feel that in my life at that

time, it was step by step. It is no use trying to force people into a spiritual experience. If you drag them into Jordan, and tow them across, they will be half drowned before they get there, and it will not be long before they are back on the other side again!

I went to meetings for the deepening of spiritual life and sometimes I would be stirred up and say, "Well, now I will lead a consecrated life; I will do better tomorrow. I won't get separated from God tomorrow. I will not allow business to come between me and my God." But when the morrow came, I was back where I was before, and felt a kind of disgust with Christian work, and inclined not to work for Christ any more. I did once or twice give myself fully to the Lord, but then the blessing seemed to pass away, only abiding perhaps while the meetings were going on or for a week or two. . . .

How was it that the blessing I sighed for at these meetings did not last? I will tell you. I did not trust in the power of God to cleanse my heart, and keep me right. I looked to myself and not to the Almighty Savior. Still by various stages I approached to the experience I was longing for.[4]

Testimonies from friends who had attended the newly opened Keswick Convention in 1884 deepened in John's heart a conviction of inner uncleanness and impotence. The testimony of E. W. Moore to having received "a clean heart," impressed him. Only Govan's own words can do justice to the glorious outcome of the fierce struggle within:

I remember the meeting where God said to me, "Here is the blessing for you." But I did not yield. The next day I was miserable. At night I went to a meeting in Salvation Hall. I went late and sat far back. I used to go to the front, but, when people are in a miserable state, they like to get to the back of a meeting.

Two friends got up and testified that they had got a clean heart. They had been at the meeting of the previous night, and something said to me, "Now, you might have had the same experience if you had just trusted." It came to the end of the meeting, and my brother called upon me to pray. I felt I had to decide there and then. Either I must refuse to pray, or I must trust the Lord to give me the blessing of a clean heart as I prayed. It happened almost in an instant. Praise the Lord, He brought me to choose the latter course, and I went down on my knees, and prayed, yielding my all to God, and trusting Him to cleanse me there and then.

I came out from that meeting and said to my friend, "I have a clean heart; I trusted the Lord, and I know He has done it, though I don't feel any different." When I got home that night and went down before the Lord, then I knew the difference. The glory of God flooded my soul, and it has been different ever since.

What a different experience it has been! Why, it was just a new life from that day! The Bible opened up to me. I enjoyed it; I saw holiness in it through and through; verse after verse spoke to my heart. I felt the truth of them, and I felt that God had brought me to know something of that truth. Hymns that I had never noticed before had new light on them. These "other lords" were all overthrown, and now I was altogether Christ's, and He was King of my heart and King of my life. Oh, do not think that the chief blessing of a clean heart is a clean heart; the chief blessing is that it is a heart in which Christ comes to reign. *It is Christ Himself Who is the chief blessing.*[5]

But Mr. Govan paid a price for this great Gift. As he testified to a clean heart, people did not like it. In fact, it was to cost him some of his friends who thought he was taking things too far. At one time, he confessed: "God has been taking me to pieces bit by bit." Yet what a change he now discovered had transpired! This transformation affected every area of his life, both inwardly and outwardly. New desires, new victory, new zeal, and new fruitfulness immediately followed.

A class which was opened for factory girls became a holiness meeting, where such a spirit of prayer prevailed that the service, which was scheduled to begin at 9.30, would often begin at 8.30 and sometimes 7.30. The fire of the Holy Ghost spread out into the streets and homes resulting in an active open-air witness for God.

Five months after this cleansing, Govan wrote:

> I yielded my heart to its rightful King, and He came in and dwells; and His kingdom, which is "righteousness, and peace, and joy in the Holy Ghost," has since then been established within. I have claimed the promise, "Ye shall abide in him," and "Whosoever abideth in him sinneth not." I trusted Him to take away all tendency, disposition, or response to sin, and I believe He has done it, according to His promise.
>
> Since then, my life in Christ has been quite different from what it was before. There has been a sense of His continual presence that I had not before, and His presence gives me a joy and peace that I knew little of previously. Of course, there is always temptation from without, but there is victory because *He is within.* And although I know there is always liability to fall, still I know there is power in Him to keep, and "I am persuaded that neither death, nor life . . . shall be able to separate us from the love of God, which is in Christ Jesus our Lord."[6]

Another secret John was learning was that in order to have the help of the Lord of the harvest in all endeavors for the lost, there must be His prescribed manner of asking His help. And that is just what prayer is ̄ a sense of our insufficiency to do the work, and an entire dependence upon God to order the method of advance. John Govan came to realize the truth of this and, in order to get more time to pray, he started rising at six o'clock as he was in business during the day, and was engaged in services practically every night in the week. But prayer was given greater emphasis than activity. On looking back on those days, Mr. Govan said: "There is one thing that stands out clearly in my mind, and that is the amount of time that we gave to prayer. Prayer became a great joy. We delighted in it. The light of God's countenance, and the atmosphere of praise and victory, were most refreshing. Whole nights of prayer were then our experience and many of our Saturday afternoons were given to prayer."[7]

Evangelistic work was now begun in the Water Street area, one of the poorest, most vice-ridden spots in Glasgow. Several of the Govan brothers became involved, and other like spirits of both sexes and of varying ages joined them. Among this little army were several who later became workers or "Pilgrims" in the Faith Mission.

The Holy Ghost is the great Initiator, and, as He was honored and consulted at all times, the advance into territory held by Satan was striking. These soldiers of the cross were willing to use any method God would reveal as His will: they waited outside the theaters to contact the dancing girls; after the public houses were closed, they brought the "drunks" into the hall for a cup of tea and a Gospel message; they marched the streets in single file with a brass band hired for the occasion.

Although Mr. Govan was satisfied with the divine work of heart cleansing, he felt, at this time, a deep longing for a greater enduement of power for service. He experienced some liberty in speaking but, as he expressed it, "not like the disciples had." At a Salvation Army half-night of prayer, an invitation was given for anyone seeking the baptism with the Holy Spirit to come to the penitent form. He went through a great struggle, wondering what people would think of his definite testimony to a clean heart. However, he went forward, confessed his need, and trusted God for the baptism with the Holy Ghost. He writes:

> I could not tell you all that the Lord did for me afterwards. It was during ten days that we set aside for prayer and waiting upon God, that He came and revealed Himself as the God of love and power in a way that I never thought possible to the soul of man. Oh, how wondrous is our God! And there has

been blessing after blessing since then, just as I needed it. I have known meetings where the Lord was in His holy temple, shedding abroad His love and His power.

One Saturday night at Water Street, we arranged to have a night of prayer, and had a wonderful outpouring of God's Holy Spirit. We commenced at ten o'clock, and we went on till six in the morning. We could not stop then, but went home for some breakfast and back again, continuing till midday. We had a wonderful time, a glorious time, a "hallelujah time." People say, "How could you go on praying for so long?" But when the Spirit of God is outpoured, there is nothing difficult or hard about prayer.[8]

In 1885, Mr. Govan gave up his business, certain that God was calling him to full-time service. Friends said he was going too far; former business associates spoke of him as "that fool, Johnny Govan." But he could only follow God's leading. Consulting with Mrs. Catherine Booth about possible personal involvement in the Salvation Army effort in India, she prophetically said that God had "some other work" for him to do. The rural areas of Scotland needed a living message, and it was doubtless God's plan for John Govan to fulfill a call which would supply this need. Meanwhile, he devoured the writings of Asa Mahan, Charles G. Finney, Mrs. Booth, and other eminent Christians and was learning well the secret of waiting upon God.

While seeking God's long-term plan for his life, he did not remain idle but began to evangelize some of the towns and villages in Scotland. Every effort was bathed in prayer, and the Holy Spirit often descended in such power in the services that it was difficult to close because of souls seeking to be right with God. Said the soul-winner:

If we are going to see souls delivered, we must get through to victory first in prayer. . . . I felt from the beginning, too, the importance of having some prayer backing, and so we formed a Prayer Union in Water Street Hall, which was the first of many hundreds. Much of the success of the work we attribute to the faithful intercession of Prayer Union members up and down the country.[9]

I have known a little of what it is to travail in birth until Christ is formed in some of these children. It has taken time and patience, and persevering prayer, but glory be to God alone we now see the result in the life and work of a lot of them.[10]

The initiation of these Prayer Unions was only a step away from the actual beginning of the Faith Mission in the following year, 1886. One other brother Pilgrim and himself represented the Mission the first twelve months. During the second year, several others were added, among them two young ladies. From this time, Mr. Govan was known as "Chief" Pilgrim, or simply the "Chief," although he always proved to be, in the words of St. Paul, "servant unto all."

Among the questions asked prospective Pilgrims were, "Are you dead to self, dead to sin, dead to the world? . . . Have you been a soul-winner at home? What have you been doing in your Prayer Union? Are you ready for anything?"[11]

Mr. Govan was convinced that each Prayer Union should be led by a man or woman "filled with the Spirit." He writes:

We feel that souls will not be saved, nor true holiness advanced merely by organizations depending on creeds, regulations, or formalism of any kind, but only as those who have the cause of Christ at heart are drawn together by the all-devouring, all-sacrificing love which animated their Master and are inspired to united action as the result of His indwelling Presence.

In too many cases where associations are upheld by many human regulations, the association manages to exist long after the Spirit has departed. And, as Christ's real kingdom is to be extended and upheld "not by might, nor by power," but by the Spirit of the living God, these spiritless gatherings are not of

God at all, but rather the opposite. May the Lord preserve the
Prayer Union meetings from any tendency to exist without
the Spirit. Better were they to die a natural death straight
away![12]

There is a progression in our knowledge of God. In her
biography of Helena Garrett, Mr. Govan's sister mentions that
her brother avoided the terms "the death of self" and "entire
sanctification" because they suggest a finality rather than a
pressing on to the "much more" which lay beyond this work of
grace. Yet this spiritual progress which John deemed so
necessary caused him to experience something of "the
fellowship of his sufferings." "A new world, spiritually," he
wrote, "the world of the Cross, seemed to dawn upon me. I
had spoken before of being of no reputation, etc., and of the
way of the Cross, but I had not experienced it like this. To be
misunderstood, mistrusted, and to go through the valley of the
shadow of death became real as part of the lot of those who
follow the Lamb."[13]

Mr. Govan, meanwhile, had become attached to Annie
Martin, one of the first two lady Pilgrims. But then it seemed
that the one he loved and whom he believed to be God's chosen
partner for him suddenly vanished from his life in a way which
bewildered and confused him. Yet almost all useful marriages
which are planned in Heaven have a waiting time‾ an element
of risk when faith is challenged as to what is really God's will.
J. G. Govan came to accept this as a reality in his own life. "I
have waited three and a half years without seeing her (Annie
Martin)," he wrote to his brother, "and can wait three and a half
more if necessary. The Kingdom of God comes first and must
remain so."[14]

Those words reveal how he was coming to know that God
is love, and any seeming withholding was only that he might
have the best. It was at this time that the invalid Annie Bowie

wrote him these encouraging lines: "How strong is the love of God. Oh the worth of His name! And amid the things that seem grievous, how we learn its value." Then she enclosed the following poem:

> "Sweep them away, and then expect the heart
>   Robbed of its choicest store,
> To give Thee all its wealth of confidence
>   To praise Thee more and more.
> 'Twere a strange venture, Lord, for Love to make
>   But that Thou knowest well,
> The vast resources of Thy mighty grace,
>   And Thine own power to heal.
> Yea, Thou art able, and I lay me down,
>   To trust and to endure;
> To kiss the Hand that either gives or takes,
>   Enriches or makes poor."[15]

At length, however, through a most unusual providence, John and Annie were brought together. The wedding took place in 1894, the young couple being confident that their love for one another, having been purified through the time of testing, was now for His glory alone.

Mr. Govan had indeed chosen wisely, for the woman of his choice proved a true helpmate, taking a mother's place, not only in their own family, but later in the Training School and Mission at large. While still very young, she had been led into the reality of Full Salvation. Her gift of song was consecrated to the Master, Who used her solos to bring sinners to Christ. And so great was the burden she carried for souls that she became known as "The Weeping Pilgrim."

Together, John and Annie Govan fought the good fight of faith. Then in the year 1909, because of failing health, they were released from responsibilities at home for a prolonged stay in South Africa. During this time, Mr. Govan's brother, Horace, took charge of the Mission and its activities. For many years he had been editor of the Mission magazine, *Bright Words.* This periodical was used in their work, and a large subscription list of 18,000 had been built up.

Within a year, the Govans, refreshed in body and soul, resumed their responsibilities in Britain. For sixteen years they had made Rothesay their headquarters, but in 1912 they moved to the outskirts of Edinburgh. Gradually they extended the work of the Mission to Ireland where they were greatly used, especially in rural areas. Even during the strenuous years of World War 1, most of the sister Pilgrims carried on much of the good work in both Scotland and Ireland and not without blessing.

Then a new door of opportunity opened to them when a friend of the Mission donated a house to be used for a Training Home for workers in the Lord's harvest field. The Govans took up residence there and it soon became apparent that the Chief was well fitted for his new post. A Japanese student said of him: "He is a very lowly man before God and men. He wants the Holy Spirit to mold the students and warriors along their own characteristics, so each one is being developed by the Holy Spirit."

Mr. Govan wisely and thoughtfully planned the curriculum of his students. "Practical work," he commented, "strips people of sentiment, supplies solidity, and helps to rub out the romantic that is apt to be a reason for some running to mission work who should have remained at home till they learned to serve God in all the details of family and business life, and do everything to His glory."

Someone has said that if an angel came down from Heaven to undertake some work for God, he would consider sweeping a street or ruling a city as of equal importance. David said, "I had rather be a doorkeeper in the house of my God, than to

dwell in the tents of wickedness." Those who have awakened
to spiritual values have likewise considered the meanest task,
if done for Christ, of equal importance with the most seemingly
impressive occupation. John Govan firmly believed this. He
wrote:

> You will generally find that fully saved people are ready
> to undertake any work, however humble, by which they can
> glorify God, such as door-keeping, selling *Bright Words,* bill-
> posting, etc. I am further of the opinion that Full Salvation
> ought to endow one with the spirit which does not only sing,
> "Fighting is a great delight," but shows itself in the life by
> willingness and eagerness to travel even miles, in fair weather
> or foul, not to be fed, but to fight, by turning up at open-airs,
> testifying, praying, dealing with souls, and giving freely of one's
> substance to help on the work.[16]

The end of Mr. Govan's earthly pilgrimage came as he
doubtless would have wished. He preached the opening sermon
at the annual convention of the Faith Mission at Perth, Scotland,
in 1927. The message was timely in the light of his soon Home-
going, for he spoke about Elijah and Elisha. The following
morning he suffered a stroke and, after three days of
unconsciousness, entered into the presence of the Lord on
October 3rd.

John G. Govan had counted not his life dear unto himself
that he might allow God to use his body as a vehicle through
which the Holy Spirit could minister to many of the large, rural
areas of Britain. Many will live to thank God for his obedience
to that call to full surrender which such a work demanded.
Surely such a man will be numbered among that select group
who "follow the Lamb whithersoever he goeth."

(Extracts from the life and writings of John G. Govan used by
permission of the Faith Mission).

Oswald Chambers

Apostle Of The Haphazard

"I feel just now," writes Oswald Chambers, "that big, never-quite-grasped idea behind our lives which must mean that God is working out His purposes. How easily it seems we might make a blunder and mar His plan, and yet I believe we are less likely to mar His plan by just going on as the days come, doing the duty that lies nearest, than by consciously trying to find it out."[1] This attitude was truly exemplified in the lives of both Oswald and Gertrude Chambers, thus enabling God to fulfill His marvelous purpose through them. This Divine plan has meant that Mr. Chamber's messages, transformed into book form, have, for more than half a century, blessed untold Christians in various parts of the globe.

Just before Oswald Chambers came upon the religious scene, books by the score had come out on holiness doctrine. Some of these were excellent, but many sadly reduced that great provision of Calvary to a mere man-defined doctrine. This often degenerated into a legal bondage to certain do's and don'ts which kept it cabined in the narrow confines of man's small mind, instead of being that living well of water springing up within a soul. Any doctrine which Christ propounded has an infinity and vastness about it which challenges all the powers of the human mind to grasp. How can a finite mind fully comprehend the infinite Mind? When you define a divine truth you limit it. However seemingly correct it may be, if void of the Holy Spirit it becomes death, or as someone aptly put it, "Straight as a gun barrel and just as cold."

In refreshing contrast, the writings of Oswald Chambers enable one to glimpse that majestic provision of Calvary for all the wants of man in the Person of the living Christ taking up His permanent abode in a heart. Through his books, the author "ruthlessly smashed through the thick plate glass of human tradition and the ignorance that had clustered round it, and found the God of love to Whom we could pray." In other words, he clarified the doctrine of holiness or sanctification which had become misty through the confused clutter of men's limited conceptions. So thorough was his Spirit-led entrance into this experience, that he brings to it many delightful aspects which make it attractive and desirable.

Oswald's first entrance into the kingdom of God when still a small boy was not after the traditional pattern, but transpired right on the street while he and his father were returning home from a service. Charles Spurgeon had been the speaker that night, and the child had confided to his father that had there been an opportunity he would have given himself to the Lord. "You can do it now, my boy," said the concerned father. And so, right then and there, as they prayed, a work of divine grace was begun that was to have tremendous consequences in the kingdom of God.

Oswald was the fourth of nine children and was born to Clarence and Hannah Chambers on July 24, 1874. His father was pastor of a Baptist Church in Aberdeen, Scotland, the city which was built with beautiful gray stone, giving it the name of the "Granite City." Oswald's parents seem to have inherited some of that granite of sturdy Scottish character and passed it on to him. They demanded a strict adherence to principle, so necessary in the development of a child's character, and yet, at the same time entered into their children's lives, often playing games with them.

Oswald's artistic and academic talent found ample scope for development when he entered Edinburgh University, and a brilliant future lay ahead of him. He occupied the same rooms in which J. H. Jowett had formerly lodged, and when his landlady pointed to the chair which had been used by that godly man, Oswald prayed that he might be imbued with the same spirit which had animated Jowett.

But his promising university career was suddenly interrupted by a Voice which he heard distinctly while tramping the hills alone one afternoon. The message was clear: "I want you in My service, but I can do without you." Here, indeed, was a divine call, and the God Who was calling him did not leave him in doubt as to where he should train for this awesome work. Upon returning to his lodgings, a brochure of a Bible Training College at Dunoon, Scotland, lay upon the table. Oswald's father, while on a trip to London, had met Mr. MacGregor, the principal of Dunoon Bible College, and had requested that some information be sent to his son. How wonderfully timed are God's providences in the lives of those He calls!

We are most fortunate to have a record of the young man's feelings at this time:

> It seems tonight that the great Spirit of God is near and all the lower common-sense things have dwindled away down into their proper proportions, and the thought that is strongest in me is that of entering the ministry. How often have I hinted at it, how often have I stifled it back and down; but I cannot keep it hid any longer for it is perplexing me tremendously. . . . This inward conviction, the decided thwarting all along the art line, nay, the repeated and pointed shutting of doors that seemed just opening, as well as the confident opinion of many friends‾ all leads me to consider most earnestly before God what is His will. I am going to leave the opening of the way in

His hands, nor am I going to try to enter the ministry until it is so startlingly clear that not to go would be to disobey.[2]

I hear continually the cry: "To what purpose is this waste?" Let my whole life be the answer for the sake of the wounded palms and feet of the Savior of the world.[3]

The father was deeply grateful upon being told of his son's final decision to give himself to the ministry. Dunoon College was the place where Oswald would get the training best fitting him for God's plan. This college had grown out of the loving heart of its principal who gathered young Christian men around him and taught them Theology, Hebrew, and Greek. It was based upon faith, so that if a young applicant had insufficient funds, he was not debarred from its privileges. The students gained practical knowledge by working on campus, and when funds were low, they prayed together for their needs to be met and received astounding answers which greatly strengthened their faith. I think it was Andrew Murray who said the subject of prayer should be included in the curriculums of Bible colleges and seminaries.

"Do not be too sorry that I cannot go in for a University curriculum," Oswald writes. "Maybe I shall be best without it. 'Seekest thou great things for thyself? Seek them not.' But although I cannot give myself a University training, I will to the limit of my power educate myself for His sake."[4]

It was while he was at Dunoon that Oswald Chambers entered into the fullness of blessing which Christ's death has purchased for everyone. A testimony to this was given at Exeter Hall in May, 1906:

After I was born again as a lad, I enjoyed the presence of Jesus Christ wonderfully, but years passed before I gave myself up thoroughly to His work. I was in Dunoon College as tutor of Philosophy when Dr. F. B. Meyer came and spoke about the Holy Spirit. I determined to have all that was going, and went to my room and asked God simply and definitely for the baptism of the Holy Spirit, whatever that meant.

From that day on for four years nothing but the overruling grace of God and the kindness of friends kept me out of an asylum. God used me during those years for the conversion of souls, but I had no conscious communion with Him. The Bible was the dullest, most uninteresting book in existence, and the sense of depravity, the vileness and bad-motivedness of my nature was terrific. I see now that God was taking me by the light of the Holy Spirit and His Word through every ramification of my being.

The last three months of those years things reached a climax, I was getting very desperate. I knew no one who had what I wanted. *IN FACT, I DID NOT KNOW WHAT I DID WANT. BUT I KNEW THAT IF WHAT I HAD WAS ALL THE CHRISTIANITY THERE WAS, THE THING WAS A FRAUD.* Then Luke 11:13 got hold of me, "If ye then, being evil, know how to give good gifts unto your children, how much more shall your heavenly Father give the Holy Spirit to them that ask Him?"

But how could I, bad-motived as I was, possibly ask for the gift of the Holy Spirit? Then it was borne in upon me that I had to claim the gift from God on the authority of Jesus Christ and testify to having done so. But the thought came⁻ if you claim the gift of the Holy Spirit on the word of Jesus Christ and testify to it, God will make it known to those who know you best how bad you are in heart. And I was not willing to be a fool for Christ's sake. But those of you who know the experience, know very well how God brings one to the point of utter despair, and I got to the place where I did not care whether everyone knew how bad I was. I cared for nothing on earth, saving to get out of my present condition.

In a little meeting held during a Mission in Dunoon, a well-known lady was asked to take the after-meeting. She did not speak, but set us to pray and then sang, "Touch Me

Again, Lord." I felt nothing, but I knew emphatically my time had come, and I rose to my feet. I had no vision of God, only a sheer, dogged determination to take God at His Word and to prove this thing for myself. And I stood up and said so.

That was bad enough, but what followed was ten times worse. After I sat down, the speaker, who knew me well, said, "That is very good of our brother. He has spoken like that as an example to the rest of you."

Up I got again and said, "I got up for no one's sake. I got up for my own sake. Either Christianity is a downright fraud, or I have not got hold of the right end of the stick." And then, and there, I claimed the gift of the Holy Spirit in dogged committal on Luke 11:13. I had no vision of Heaven or of angels. I had nothing. I was as dry and empty as ever, no power or realization of God, no witness of the Holy Spirit.

Later I was asked to speak at a meeting, and forty souls come out to the front. Did I praise God? No, I was terrified and left them to the workers, and went to Mr. MacGregor and told him what had happened. He said, "Don't you remember claiming the Holy Spirit as a gift on the word of Jesus, and that He said, 'Ye shall receive power. . .'? This is the power from on high." And, like a flash, something happened inside me, and I saw that I had been wanting power in my hand, so to speak, that I might say, "Look what I have got by putting my all on the altar."

If the previous years had been Hell on earth, these four years have truly been Heaven on earth. Glory be to God, the last aching abyss of the human heart is filled to overflowing with the love of God. Love is the beginning, love is the middle, and love is the end. After He comes in, all you see is "Jesus only, Jesus ever."

The baptism of the Holy Ghost (he said afterwards), does not make you think of time or eternity, it is one amazing, glorious now. . . . It is no wonder that I talk so much about an altered disposition: God altered mine; I was there when He did it, and I have been there since.[5]

You ask a question (he explained at another time) about the baptism of the Holy Ghost⁻ did I get there all at once, or easily? No I did not. Pride and the possession of the high esteem of my many Christian friends kept me out for long enough. But immediately I was willing to sacrifice all and put myself on the Altar, which is Jesus Himself, all was begun and done.

Holiness is not an attainment at all, it is the gift of God, and the pietistic tendency is the introspection which makes me worship my own earnestness and not take the Lord seriously at all. It is a pious fraud that suits the natural man immensely. *He makes holy, He sanctifies, He does it all. All I have to do is to come as a spiritual pauper, not ashamed to beg, to let go of my right to myself and act on Romans 12: 1-2.* It is never *"Do, do,* and you'll be with the Lord," but *"Be, be,* and I will *do* through you." It is a case of "hands up" and letting go, and then entire reliance on Him.[6]

During this time, Oswald knew terrible onslaughts when slanders of all kinds assailed him. Only the loving understanding of the Principal and Mrs. MacGregor enabled him to ride through this stormy period without faltering.

Wonderful as had been his experience, this new man with the indwelling Christ did not think, as so many do, that his seeking had now ended. There was much more out there. His horizon had widened. There were continents of grace to be explored. In his books he pleads with those who feel they have attained to grace, to study diligently through the Bible to discover what it is that God has done for their souls. "Sanctify your sanctification," he insisted when dealing with others. Had he seen how holiness had been degraded by many who thought of it as a mere "IT" rather than a "HE"⁻ an attainment of something which, when once possessed, its owner thinks of himself as being rather superior, and so becomes smug and self-righteous? Oswald had discovered for himself that the end of sanctification is that we might glorify Jesus with every ransomed power.

In his book, *Not Knowing Whither,* he makes a very important but little understood distinction between our sinful self, and our natural self:

> When we are born again we enthrone Ishmael, that is, we consecrate our natural gifts and say these are the things with which God is going to do His work: they are the things God makes His servants, and I have to see that they are put in the position of servants. If I put them on the throne, I start a mutiny within my own soul. The bondwoman and her child have to be cast out; the natural has to be sacrificed in order that it may be brought into perfect at-home-ness with the Spirit of God. If we make our natural life submit and obey the Holy Spirit within us, we will hasten the time for the manifestation of the sons of God (Rom. 8:21). It is the man who can rule his natural spirit that is able to take the city. It is only when we have learned to bring the natural life into perfect submission to the ruling personality of God that God dare turn His saints loose. It is of no use to turn out a lot of "half-baked Ephraims" into unlimited power.[7]

Now Mr. Chambers' sphere of influence began to be enlarged. He had witnessed in his spiritual Jerusalem, and the time had come when he was to witness for Christ further afield. In 1905 he went as a delegate from Perth to a League of Prayer Conference, where he met Reader Harris who became a tremendous help to him. Here he also met a Japanese Christian, Bishop Nakada, with whom he felt an immediate bond. They took services together in the north of Scotland, and then traveled to the U.S.A. where they visited God's Bible School at Cincinnati. Eventually their itinerary took them to Japan.

In 1910, at thirty-six years of age, he was united in marriage to Gertrude Hobbs, who had been a member of his brother Arthur's church. A year later, the young couple was asked to open a Bible College in Clapham, London, in connection with the League of Prayer. He speaks of this time as being the very "Gate of Heaven" to them. "These four years at the B. T. C.," said Oswald Chambers, "have been unique and blessed, and they terminate in a quiet, unobtrusive, splendid, and final way."[8]

It was the world conflict of 1914 which changed the entire course of Oswald's life. He wrote: "Since the war began, it has been a pressure on me all but unendurable to be here, but I know God well enough not to confound my own natural desires and impulses for His will or ordering. . . . At New Year time as Biddy and I waited before God, I said to her, 'Just look at my verse⁻ "I am now ready to be offered."'"[9]

The door of opportunity eventually opened and he took a post under the auspices of the Y.M.C.A. as a Chaplain to the Forces in Zeitoun, Egypt. In letters to his parents, he told them of how definite was the call to minister spiritual first-aid to men at the front, many of whom might never return, while others might be maimed for life.

Down through the centuries there has always been a noble company composed of individuals who have left home and loved ones for the lonely, isolated outposts where needy souls required the message of God's great Redemptive plan. These are those who "follow the Lamb whithersoever he goeth." These are committed to obedience, and their ears are attune to the Master of the Vineyard. Oswald Chambers truly belonged to this company, for he left the trodden path of service for the trackless desert. Boundless horizons lay before the indefatigable Chaplain as he expresses it in his poetry written while still a student in Edinburgh:

"Let me climb, let me climb, I'm sure I've time
    'Ere the mist comes up from the sea,
Let me climb in time to the height sublime;
    Let me reach where I long to be.

"Oh, I'm tired and spent, but I seek the peak
    In the sun glare, strong and wild⁻
Now I've reached the top⁻ but the thing I seek
    Is hid⁻ and I cry like a child."[9]

For the next two years he was to prepare and give lectures five nights a week, one evening being devoted to questions and problems presented. Sunday night a general evangelistic meeting was in order.

From diary, letters, and extracts from lectures we realize what caused Oswald Chambers to mature so early. A man's prayer life is in exact proportion to a sense of his own insufficiency. Without prayer, we only get what man can do, but a man who walks and talks with Divinity has something other-worldly about all he does. This was the secret of the life of this servant of God in this respect. He tells us:

> What a great thing prayer is. I am sure God's generous sovereignty and the earnest prayers of the saints are the only reason I am used as I am. . . . The life of God in us is manifested by spiritual concentration, not by pious self-consciousness; pious self-consciousness produces the worship of prayer, which is anti-Christian. This unscriptural piety fixes itself on the actual incidents in such verses as Mark 1:35, "And in the morning, rising up a great while before day, he went out, and departed into a solitary place, and there prayed," and disproportionately emphasizes "rising up a great while before day," implying that if this actual early rising were imitated it would produce Christ-likeness in us; whereas our Lord prayed

because He was concentrated on God; that is, He did not worship prayer.

The early morning hours of prayer are unspeakably fine. I go over the camp and the men, and never cease to ask God to charge the atmosphere of the Hut with His Spirit, and that prayer is answered in the certain restraint on language and conduct. I cannot convey what a fathomless rest this intercession on behalf of the men is. . . . Now I go into the day watching God's great ways again.[10]

The following statement of Chambers helped us some years ago to better understand the true purpose of communion with God:

One of the most helpful ideas in your life is to remember that the life of the Son of God in us is nourished by prayer and devotion. When we neglect prayer and devotion, we may not suffer, but His life in us is starved. You catch the idea? In every crisis consider neither yourself nor others as primary, but only your relationship to Him.

I have just talked to the men on "What's the good of Prayer?" and thank God, the room was packed. My main point was not so much that prayer alters things, but rather that prayer alters men that they may alter things.[11]

As we obey the leadings of the Spirit of God, we enable God to answer the prayers of other people. I mean that our lives, my life, is the answer to someone's prayer, prayed perhaps centuries ago. It is more and more impossible to me to have programs and plans because God alone has the plan, and our plans are only apt to hinder Him and make it necessary for Him to break them up.[12]

How unproselytizing God is! I feel the "soul winning" campaign is often at heart the apotheosis of commercialism, the desire to see so much result from so much expenditure. The ordinary evangelical spirit is less and less congenial to my own soul; the vastness of the ministry of intercession is, and the willingness to testify to the hope that is in you, and to stir up people to think, and to take the apparently haphazard opportunities of talking personally to people about what you have discovered of God.

Being such a man of prayer, it is little wonder that his writings are full of the subject:

Every saint of God knows those times when in closest communion with God nothing is articulated, and yet there seems to be an absolute intimacy not so much between God's mind and their mind as between God's Spirit and their spirit.

When the goads of the Almighty are in a man or a work, God prospers that man or that work mightily.[13]

The prayer of the feeblest saint on earth who lives in the Spirit and keeps right with God is a terror to Satan. The very powers of darkness are paralyzed by prayer; no spiritualistic séance can succeed in the presence of a humble praying saint. No wonder Satan tries to keep our minds fussy in active work till we cannot think in prayer. It is a vital necessity for Christians to think along the lines on which they pray. The philosophy of prayer is that prayer is *the* work.

March 22. A great fear has been at work in my mind, and God has used it to rouse me to prayer. I came across a man whom I knew years ago, a mighty man of God, and now ten years have gone and I met him again⁻ garrulous and unenlivened. How many men seem to become like that after forty years of age! The fear of sloth and indulgence has come home with a huge fear and fairly driven me to God to keep me from ever forgetting what I owe Him.[14]

I have good times at the throne for you all, morning by morning. God bless you. It does take some pluck and courage, doesn't it, to refuse to take the pattern and print of the religious age one lives in.[15]

His brother Ernest's remembrance of Oswald was that of a praying man. He couched it in poetic language:

> "Prayer was to him the very breath of life,
>   Like early morning dew,
> His prayers rose daily up before the shrine
> For you and yours, for all, for me and mine.
> He was as 'broken bread and poured out wine'
>   For everyone he knew."[16]

From his early days at the College, Oswald hated notoriety or publicity. "Everything goes with me in amazing prosperity," he writes. "Perhaps the consciousness that I am thought of too highly makes me want to get away at times. They all place me so high that I am weary of it. Oh that I might be away with Nature, and see and not be seen."

At another time he observed: "It is our whole work of faith to take up the obscure tasks within ourselves which we know must be attended to if we are to live on happy terms with Jesus Christ our Lord."

His intensity of desire to be like Christ absorbed him:

> I am hungry with a vast desire for Him. As I go about for Him other lives seem to me to get clearer and clearer, but I find I dare not look to anyone to understand mine. This is not pride, but the call is on me, intolerably strong at times. I am full of joy always, but a tremendous sorrow seems to be interwoven with it all. I seem to hear Him, but still I am dense and dark to His meaning. I wish He would take me into His counsel or let me live on the lower level. I am just sensitive enough to His Spirit to know that we are on the eve of new things, not the revival that everyone seems to be talking about, that does not appeal to me. Nor is it the Second Coming. I know He is coming again, and coming again soon. But there

is something He wants me to see and know, and I seem stupid. I can feel intuitively the Spirit of God striving with me, but it is all inarticulate. . . .

I see churches and schemes and missionary enterprises, and holiness movements, all tagged with His Name and how little of Himself! I wish every breath I drew, all speech I made, could make Him come and seem more real to men. Nothing is worth living for but just Himself.[17]

Thus far, we have not said anything about Oswald's conviction that suffering was an integral part of our being fashioned and molded into the image of the Son. We quote a number of his reflections:

By the depth of my sorrow shall be my capacity to sympathize. Sympathy at times is a direct form of selfishness, at other times it is the divinest capacity of our human nature. Oh for more of that Christ-like courage to smite rather than caress! And yet, oh for more sympathy with really weak, halting characters. God knows how to pity them, characters so weak that they can never be strong. Jesus Christ looks out for the weak ones whom the world shoves to the wall. He puts His back to the wall and receives them into His arms.

. . .You may wonder that I have not said anything about suffering as playing a great part in the making of holy, patient ones: but do I need to refer to the night when I speak of the sunrise? Do I need to tell you of the blazing, fiery furnace when I speak of the pure gold? Do I need to tell you of the quarry blast or the mallet and chisel when I speak of the statue? Then surely, I need not remind you of suffering when I speak of holy patience, or that Jesus said, "If any man will come after me, let him deny himself, and take up his cross, and follow me."

Jesus Christ foretold tribulation: He conveyed His message with a clarion voice to the saints in all ages: "In the world ye shall have tribulation," and the Apostle Paul continually warns us that we have no right to settle on our lees. "For verily, when we were with you, we told you plainly that we are to suffer affliction; even as it came to pass, and ye know." Tribulation means being thronged by severe affliction and trouble; that is what the saints are to expect in this dispensation and not be astonished when it comes.

God allows tribulation and anguish to come right to the threshold of our lives in order to prove to us that His life in us is more than a match for all that is against us. When we see the awfulness of evil in this world we imagine there is no room for anything but the devil and wrong; but this is not so. God restrains the powers of evil. How does He do it? Through the lives of the saints who are pushing the battle everywhere their feet are placed. The devil tackles on the right hand and on the left but they are more than conquerors, they not only go through the tribulation, but are "exceeding joyful" in it.

At only 43 years of age, undiagnosed appendicitis which resulted in peritonitis in November, 1917, caused the transfer of Oswald Chambers from his earthly warfare to his eternal furlough. He had been designated to go to the front, but God thought differently and took him to His heavenly home-front to be forever with the One Whom he had served so faithfully and intensely.

His brother wrote a tribute at his death. We quote several stanzas of the poem:

> "The daily miracle of rising sun
> To him was keen delight.
> What must his glorified emotion be
> Within that City of infinity
> That needs no sun to orient majesty,
> For God Himself's the Light?

"Heaven lent him to us for a little while,
       Thank God, we loved him well,
But He had need of him in worlds more blest.
Now, 'midst God's hosts he waits his King's behest;
'Thy will be done,' in this our spirits rest.
For we believe and say¯ that God knows best
       Who doeth all things well."[18]

The truest test of man's life as to whether he has labored in the Spirit or in the flesh is worded so well by Phillips Brooks that we quote him here: "This is the difference between men whose power stops with their death, and those whose power really opens into its true richness when they die. The first sort of men have mechanical power; the second have spiritual power. The final test and witness of spiritual force is the ability to cast the bodily life away and yet continue to give help and courage to those who see us no longer; to be, like Christ, the helper of men's souls¯ even from beyond the grave."[19]

By that standard, Oswald Chambers was indeed a spiritual man. Fifty-eight years after his death, an advert was sent to us by his publishers, Marshall Morgan and Scott, saying, "The messages of Oswald Chambers in the many books bearing his name today enjoy an even wider readership than ever. The half-dozen reprints have just come from the press, bringing the total number of copies of his books printed this year to 185,500¯ eloquent evidence that the challenging words of this saintly man continue to command attention in today's world."

Gertrude Chambers

MAKER OF BOOKS

We have heard much of Oswald Chambers through his books which have had a powerful effect upon the Christian reading public, but we know little of the woman behind the scenes who made these publications possible. Recently, however, several of those working on the staff of Harvey and Tait Publications had an interview with her daughter, Kathleen Chambers, who is living in London. She very graciously gave information about her mother which we recorded and wish to pass on in this sketch. The quotations we have used from Kathleen have received little editing and are printed much as they were spoken so that the meaning of her words remains unaltered.

It is most fascinating to see how God, in His foresight, prepared an instrument to preserve the secrets of the Lord as revealed to Oswald Chambers. One stands amazed to trace His hand moving purposefully but quietly and unobserved amidst the chaos and seeming meaninglessness of this world's scene of action in order to bring about His divine will. The Bible often speaks of this moving of God's hand on behalf of His chosen people.

Rarely can we realize, in our short-sightedness, the loving kindness of God in those providences which appear to thwart us in our plans. When a child of thirteen, Gertrude Hobbs developed severe bronchitis which meant that she had to spend three months of every year in bed. Doubtless she must have wondered "why me?" when she would hear the voices of her school-mates as they passed along the street, unhampered by ill-health and living the normal, active life of a teenager.

This chronic ill-health led to a further distressing circumstance. Gertrude's grandmother and grandfather were in the bakery business and doing quite well, when, because of a partner who did not "play the game," they became bankrupt. Being an invalid, the grandmother had to have someone stay at home with her. After consultation, the family decided to choose Gertrude, seeing that she already had missed so much schooling. Just as she was blooming into womanhood and able to appreciate everything to the full, the cherished education was once more denied her.

But the young girl's desire for knowledge had to find its vent somehow. At fifteen, she had the ambition to one day become the secretary to the Prime Minister. She knew that this would mean becoming proficient in shorthand so she obtained Pittman's correspondence course and studied it eagerly. Her grandmother and aunt would read aloud to her, and so her dictation speed improved and eventually reached 250 words per minute. "She had to be perfection," said her daughter, "for the characteristic of her life was to be the best."

Now fully equipped, she entered the business world and became secretary to the Major General of Woolwich Arsenal; later she worked for a barrister, doing all his briefs. Then a position as secretary to one of the directors of Thomas Houston's firm in New York became open. Gertrude applied and was accepted and worked there for two or three years.

It was at this period in her life that Gertrude met the man whom she was to marry. To quote her daughter: "She came back to England. My uncle, who was the minister at her church, used to be away at times, so my father would come and take the services in his absence. So my mother got to know my father because the family entertained him on Sundays. Mother thought my father was way up there, you know, and wouldn't sort of think of anybody at all as far as marriage was concerned."

When Gertrude Hobbs decided to return to America, providence would have it that Oswald Chambers had several speaking engagements over there as well, and so they traveled on the same steamship. It was during this trip that they entered into an engagement with one another. Later, they would both take outings to the Catskill Mountains, when Oswald would dictate to her the contents of his two books on the Disciplines of Guidance, Peril, etc. which now appear in two volumes. So even before they were married, they had already begun their publishing venture.

The wedding took place on May 25, 1910, just a few months before Oswald's thirty-sixth birthday. Unknown to neither bride nor groom, their married life would be brief‾ only seven years' duration.

Their first appointment came through the Pentecostal League of Prayer, when the young couple was asked to initiate a Bible College at Clapham Common. "It was an unusual Bible College," Kathleen said. "It was open to anybody and everybody who had a mind to come, and the only rule in the whole of the college was: 'Please leave this room as you found it.'" Then she related a fascinating incident her mother had told her about life at the college:

> They had in the kitchen a man and his wife who had come to do the cooking. They had been a butler and a housekeeper in one of the big houses in the neighborhood. They had no job at the time, so they were both taken on as cook and sort of general manager of the college. A very dear friend of ours, who was helping in the kitchen, came to my mother one day and said, "I'm very perturbed, you know, because things are disappearing‾ blankets as well as food and all sorts of things. It's obvious who is doing it."

Hearing about this, my father advised, "Don't do anything about it. We'll just tell God and leave it completely." So these things went on disappearing.

Eventually the man went to my father, very cut-up and broken down, and said, "I want to tell you I am ashamed that my wife and I have been consistently taking things from your linen and store cupboards ever since your college opened. I can't bear the thought that I have taken in you good people."

My father replied, "You haven't taken us in. We knew you were doing it, but we wanted God's Spirit to tell you." My mother said the man was completely overcome and both he and his wife came to a very deep and real knowledge of God. My mother always felt this was such a wonderful lesson to learn. God can do something so much more effectively in His own way than if we step in clumsily and try to stop something.

It was during this time at the College that Gertrude felt an impelling "must" to take everything down in shorthand that her husband said in lectures or in services. Thus began the collection of material for all his books.

In the midst of her busy life, a little daughter, Kathleen, was born. Gertrude had such a difficult time at her birth that she was cautioned not to have any more children.

Meanwhile, low-hanging clouds were threatening Britain and it was not long before the storm broke, plunging the nation into a war which would influence the lives of many, including the Chambers family, for Oswald decided to become a chaplain to the forces in Egypt and to run a hut for the Y.M.C.A. in Cairo. It was decided that Gertrude and Kathleen would not accompany him then but follow later. When the time came for them to leave, the vessel on which they were eventually scheduled to sail did not have accommodation for them. It seemed, at the time, another hindering circumstance. But not so; it was nothing less than the moving hand of God's providence protecting both wife and child, for the boat on which they would have sailed was sunk!

Safely reunited at last, Gertrude was not long in engaging in the work enthusiastically. Once more she would take her shorthand notebook to preserve for posterity Oswald's lectures to the soldiers.

Kathleen again reveals her father's unique way of working. "Formerly the Y.M.C.A. workers would take advantage of the Sunday meal to afterwards speak to the men, but my father did not feel to work like this. He said, 'No, they've gone in there to eat, and if they want to hear about God afterwards, all right.' Consequently the hut that we had the meetings in afterwards was chock-a-block with men standing inside and outside."

Unknown to them, the brief years which Gertrude and her husband were to spend together were fast coming to a close. After only two years in Egypt, Oswald took seriously ill. He had an undiagnosed appendicitis which turned into peritonitis. Gertrude accompanied him to the hospital in order to stay with him and took a room there. In her distress over her husband's illness, she had received a verse which was a comfort to her: "This sickness is not unto death, but for the glory of God," and she interpreted that to mean that her husband would rally. The nursing sister shook her head when the hopeful wife told her this, saying, "No. It's quite impossible. Quite impossible. Your husband cannot live through this. He cannot live through this."

And so, at only forty-three years of age, Oswald Chambers died early one November morning in 1917 contrary to all Gertrude's expectations. We can only imagine the grief that was hers and yet, with a daughter only four years old, the brave wife nobly took up the work her husband had laid down. Faithfully she would take the services with the men in the hut, perhaps not yet realizing that her true life work was just about to begin.

"Other people told me," Kathleen said, "that nobody ever saw my mother crying. She always believed that what He allowed to happen and what He sent meant that He was there anyway all the time. She was never sorry or sad, feeling that God had made a mistake because my father was at the beginning of his life. She told me that I always took it very well because you see I was only four and when she told me that my father had died, (she did cry with me), I said, 'Why are you crying? He's gone to be with Jesus.'"

The publication of her husband's books began in a seemingly haphazard manner. A friend suggested to Mrs. Chambers, "Why don't you send out a Christmas card or a New Year's card to all the people who knew him." And so Gertrude started by getting something from her notes. She then realized that she had collected a cabin trunk full of shorthand books containing all the lectures that her husband had given in America, at the College, and now in Egypt. This resulted in her getting some small books printed in America through the Nile Press.

With the breadwinner gone, it must indeed have been a testing time for Gertrude. A return to England was inevitable but finances were low. It is a compliment to the Chambers that they never made merchandise of the business of winning souls to Christ. Many have used the Gospel as a means of accruing personal benefits to themselves. Gertrude now had to put into effect Oswald's principle of trusting in the Lord alone for all her needs. Had her husband not said that one had to be poured out wine in order to bless others and had he not felt that the prophet must first work out in his own life the message he would eventually give to others? Now his widow and fatherless child were thrust upon the God Whom their loved one had so faithfully served with no thought of personal gain.

Upon their arrival in Britain, they went to stay with very old friends in Finsbury Park in England who gladly shared their apartment with them. Kathleen tells us:

> My mother wonderfully then wrote a diary in longhand for about three years, which she usually never did (everything she did was in shorthand) and I found them a long time after she died. I was surprised to see I could read them. . . . Eventually we found a little cottage outside Oxford which was right in the country⁻ no electricity and no water laid on. We paid five shillings a week for it and a friend of ours, Miss Ash, and my mother and I lived there. I used to walk across the fields and get the train to school.

For a time, Biddy, as Oswald Chambers used to call his wife, went on the Methodist Plan (a system whereby lay preachers would take turns filling local pulpits). She would go out into the village churches. But when a large, old house was procured, she was able to board four Oxford university students. "It was then that my mother started to type *My Utmost For His Highest*," Kathleen tells us. "She had a basement room and typed on the *Utmost* every day. That's how *My Utmost* came to be, when she was working about twelve hours a day, cooking, and shopping with very little money, but they were wonderfully happy days."

Gertrude became her own publisher, the finance being met by her faith in God and the gifts of loving friends. Everything that was sold was put immediately into the fund for more books. Nobody helped her in making corrections or proof-reading. She began to feel that God was going to use the books and extend her husband's influence. The promise, "This sickness is not unto death," was being fulfilled.

When another move became necessary, Gertrude, accompanied of course by her daughter, went to live with her mother and sisters in Muswell, London. Her sisters, by taking care of the mother, relieved her to work on the books. The Lord provided a wonderful publisher for them, Simpkin Marshall, who though not a religious publisher, had tremendous business opportunities and soon put Oswald Chambers' books on the London bookstands, bus stations, and other public places.

When Gertrude's mother died, the sisters decided to move as the house was too large. It was then, in 1935, that Gertrude and Kathleen took up residence permanently at Woodberry Crescent. All through the Second World War they lived there, and servicemen knocking at their door felt sure of a welcome, for Gertrude Chambers was truly given to hospitality. Her side door was never locked day or night. One wonders how she could possibly have gotten thirty-one books ready for the press while lavishly entertaining nine or ten people every day of the week.

The books, too, brought more visitors, for those who had been helped through reading them wanted to call on her, and those who came were never turned aside. When Kathleen, who by now was nursing, would return home from work, she would find the house full of people. Soldiers and sailors would greet her with: "We've been here all day and your mother told us to stay for supper, so we're trying to find the things to lay the table with, you see."

"One thing I remember very well about my mother," said Kathleen, "was that she always got up very early in a morning and had her time with God. If she was interrupted, it was all right with her. She gave us all cups of tea in bed and thin pieces of bread and butter. . . . My mother would never pre-arrange who was going to come for the day. She would put the day in God's hands and ask Him to overrule completely whatever happened."

American servicemen who had no relatives in Britain would also be welcomed to the home. And when Kathleen had a Bible class in the east end, Mrs. Chambers would invite these poor children to have Christmas with them. Kathleen told one story which illustrates her mother's character very well:

> We had a very ugly "over mantel" in the lounge which had to be taken down. My mother said, "We should have a picture on there. Let's go to London and get a picture." So we went up to Trafalgar Square where there was a very beautiful art gallery. We saw a beautiful picture, but it was much more money than we meant to spend. Even so we bought the picture and Mother said, "Let's go and have a cup of coffee in the coffee house." After a drink, Mother suggested, "Let's go home by taxi." I objected that we had not enough money. "Never mind," she said, "let's go home by taxi."
>
> Upon opening her purse to the taxi man, she said, "Look, this is all the money I've got and we live in Muswell Hill. Now take us as far as you can for this money and leave us with enough to get the bus for the rest of the way." This was just my mother being very open.
>
> Obviously the man brought us all the way home. He came back in our dining room and had tea with us, and Mother showed him the books. He was so impressed; but you see that's a difficult story to tell because it looks as if she had an ulterior motive in what she did, which was not the case. That man came to know God and he had a lot of books from us which, of course, were given to him.

Then there came the time when Gertrude Chambers took ill and was unable to finish any more books. Perhaps her program had been too heavy. Her output, certainly, had been colossal. She had typed thirty-one volumes of her husband's messages and had started the thirty-second when she died in 1966. There are still unpublished notes on Isaiah and a few on Jeremiah and Ezekiel.

Gertrude had come to learn through experience, as her husband had done, that God never coddles His saints. Living in a world antagonistic to the Gospel of Christ, they are often allowed to feel the attacks of the evil one. When London was so terribly bombed in the last war, the Chambers' publications were not exempt. Fire bombs destroyed 40,000 volumes. This disaster showed how plucky Mrs. Chambers was, for, undeterred, she reprinted every one!

In the great beyond when spiritual results are tabulated, husband and wife will share in the gracious "Well done, good and faithful servants." We can never fathom how much we owe to Oswald Chambers for his depth of spiritual perception and understanding of the mysteries of the kingdom. He put his very life-blood into his message, and that always comes through to us in his writings. To Gertrude Chambers we also owe a tremendous debt of gratitude for the many hours of daily toil and concentrated effort, which no one has any conception of save those who, like her, have prepared manuscripts for the printer. We are grateful for the Spirit's impulse which prompted her to take everything down in shorthand. She is doubtless seeing now with undimmed vision the Father's loving-kindness in what seemed cruel. She can trace His hand in allowing her to suffer that chronic bronchitis which kept her from regular schooling in order that she might have the time to become adept in shorthand. What other specialized training could have made her such an effectual conveyer and preserver of truths for the Church invisible!

Evan Hopkins

MESSENGER OF VICTORY

It was only a tuft of grass growing on the edge of a crag but it stood between young Evan Hopkins and certain death. It must have appeared to the eyes of the frightened, young English engineer as a life buoy would appear to a drowning man, or as a fireman's ladder would loom up to one trapped in an upper story of a burning building.

Sitting on the slope above the cliff and enjoying the fine view of the Isle of Man coast, Evan had suddenly realized that he was slipping toward the fatal edge. In vain he frantically tried with his hands and feet to stop the downward slide but the short, dried grass was so slippery that he could obtain neither foothold nor handhold. And then to his desperate gaze there had appeared this saving tuft of green which, to his deepest gratitude, held as he planted one foot against it. He lay trembling for some moments trying to regain his equilibrium in this precarious position. Finally he managed to get one boot up to his hands and unlace it. Holding on then with that foot he took the boot off the other and struggling and turning in his stocking-soles, he was then able to get just enough hold to make his way slowly to safety.

Could this deliverance have been the answer to the prayers of his godly Methodist hosts whom he had accidentally heard praying for the spiritual awakening of their young lodger? Doubtless it was all a link in the chain of wonderful providences which were surrounding this young man, so that he might one day become a special messenger to despairing and defeated Christians the world over.

Evan Henry Hopkins had been born in New Granada, an island situated in the Caribbean Sea, and was the son of a well-traveled engineer who had planned mines and other industrial constructions in various parts of the world. The father had taken this promising son with him to Australia where the lad had finished the last four years of his education. The older Hopkins, a scientist as well as an engineer, desired that his son should follow in his own footsteps, not realizing that there was One Whose immense love would have higher claims upon his son than any father could possess.

Growing up, Evan seems to have had serious thoughts about the things of God and eternity. He was confirmed in the Church of England but his soul remained unawakened to eternal matters. Then he had been sent to the Isle of Man on his first assignment as an engineer and lodged with Mr. Summers, a Methodist and a humble servant of Christ. One evening when Evan had been about to attend a certain party, he had warned him against participating in anything unworthy of a Christian. Evan had answered that common sense would be his safety. "But no," was the reply, "it is not common sense; it is the grace of God."[1]

The Providence which saved his life that memorable day made Evan think but did not immediately lead him to a complete trust in Christ. At the age of twenty-four, the young engineer moved from the Isle of Man to Kimmersridge, a village in Dorset on the mainland. There, when a mine over which he had presided for a time was closed, Evan took over the management of the extensive property of a wealthy landowner.

One evening, one of the local coastguardsmen with whom he had struck up a friendship, surprised Evan by exclaiming, "I have served the devil for forty years; but I mean now to serve the Lord Jesus Christ."[2] He told how, while alone the day before, the words, "The blood of Jesus Christ his Son cleanseth us from all sin," had come to him most forcibly. Then and there he had given himself completely to the Savior. On the beach, in the moonlight, the new convert had asked Hopkins to pray. He tried but gave it up and listened instead while the other humbly spoke to his new-found Master.

Deep gratitude came into Evan's heart as he realized that he was in the presence of a converted man. Awe-struck, he made his way to his lodgings and with deep solemnity said to his sister who was anxious about his long absence, "Don't say anything. I have met a truly converted man." On the following Tuesday, in response to an invitation, he went to the home of his new friend to enquire further about this wonderful event called conversion. He was startled to find a room full of coastguardsmen and their wives, and to learn that he was expected to hold a service for them. He writes of this occasion and of its life-changing consequences as follows:

I said, "This is too bad of you, Harnden. I never undertook to do this."

"Never mind," he replied, "come along with me, sir," and he led me into a little ante-room, and prayed, "We may not all be able to say, 'Come to Jesus,' but we can all pray that we may go to Jesus together, and not be afraid of men or ashamed of Him."

We then went into the meeting. I had not a word to say, but I took a little book from my pocket, which had the Lord's Prayer on the back. I spread it on the table, and, after singing a hymn, we repeated the prayer. Next I called on Harnden to pray. He said, "I should like to say a word first. Fellow boatmen, you know what a rough, wild man I have been, cruel to my wife, and a careless fellow; but I have served the devil for forty years, and now I mean to serve the Lord Jesus Christ." Then we knelt and he poured out his heart in confession.

After another hymn, I was supposed to give an address. While the singing was going on, I tried to think of something to speak about. I recollected a sermon I had heard some years before at St. James's, Ramsgate, from Archdeacon Davies, a preacher who had been an actor. His text was, "Jonah was exceeding glad." I said to myself, "I will give them what I remember of that." One difficulty was that I did not recollect in what part of the Bible the Book of Jonah was; but, just before the hymn concluded, I found it. I described the difference between being glad and being thankful; how the latter pointed to grace and to God. I was beginning to feel that I had nothing more for them, when Harnden said, "Shall we have a word of prayer?" I was relieved at this, and he prayed; and I just closed with the benediction. I had never been at such a meeting in my life. . . .

For about a fortnight, I was in great anxiety of soul; but on Monday, Feb. 20th, I was reading in my room aloud the verse, "If we confess our sins, he is faithful and just to forgive us our sins, and to cleanse us from all unrighteousness." I said to God, "Lord, I cannot see this. If it were written, 'Thou art gracious and merciful to forgive,' I could understand; but how canst Thou be faithful and just to forgive: faithful to whom? Just to whom? Now, Lord, show me."

I was longing for life and peace. Well, before I rose from my knees, the whole thing was made clear to me. I saw that there was a covenant, not between God and man, but between God and Christ. If I was among those who confessed their sins, I was in the agreement, and then He was faithful to the Son, and just to the promise made to the Son to forgive me then and there. I saw at once that I had pardon; and peace came into my soul. I asked Mr. Reeve, the Rector, if this was sound and he said, "O yes, it is sound."[3]

That this young man was born again⁻ a new creature in Christ Jesus⁻ there could be no doubt either to himself or to those who knew him best. When we remember that Evan Hopkins was a communicant in the Church of England where the clergy are highly educated and the services are performed in order and decorum, we realize the truth that God had once more used the base things, the weak things, to bring about His divine purposes.

Evan was now overflowing with a new life. His ambitions were changed along with everything else. Although his prospects in the field of applied and practical science had been rosy, he now turned his face toward another goal. He would preach this wonderful Gospel story that had now come to mean so much to him. First to his newly-made friends, the coastguardsmen, and then to all he met, the young man witnessed clearly and courageously.

It happened to be the year 1859 when the spirit of revival was abroad. Evan was soon taking people individually by name before his heavenly Father. He early learned a perseverance that would not give up the case until an assurance was given that his Father had heard. To the disappointment of Mr. Hopkins Sr., he abandoned all plans along the engineering line and, instead, studied for the ministry. Ordained in the Church of England, he became a missionary curate in the London docks' area.

In 1871, this young curate married Isabella Sarah Kitchen, whose godly mother had taken her to house meetings such as those held in the home of Lady Radstock. Deeply convicted for sin, Isabella, too, had been transformed by the grace of God. She was truly fitted to be the life-partner Evan needed. Together the young couple, full of love and zeal for souls, began their married life in Richmond, very near to London proper where he had been inducted as Vicar of St. John's Parish.

The Salvation Army was in those days hot on the attack for souls. Mr. Hopkins and his wife adopted and adapted many of the Army's despised but successful tactics such as knee-drill, open air meetings, marches, banners, brass bands, etc. This parish really became the birthplace of the Church Army, later developed by Wilson Carlisle who with his wife and sister learned their first spiritual lessons under Mr. Hopkins' earnest ministry.

Sincere and devoted in his service for God, Evan was approaching that point in his personal history when he would discover the secret which was to lift his life from the plane of the "in-and-out," "up-and-down," and "ebb-and-flow" of the Christian life as he afterwards would describe it. He had recently devoured a book by Dr. Boardman, *The Higher Christian Life,* and had been much moved by its contents only to have his personal hopes of attainment dashed by the warning of a fellow-clergyman that its teaching was "dangerous and quixotic."

But the subject of victorious living did not lie dormant long. It was brought into the Vicarage by a minister who was residing there while conducting services in the Parish. This visitor frequently discussed the papers on holiness by Robert Pearsall Smith. These taught that Full Salvation included not only emancipation from the guilt of past sins but provided, through faith in Calvary's sacrifice, freedom from the inner power of evil which every child of Adam knew, whether it was concealed beneath the laborer's apron or the clergyman's gown. This message challenged Mr. Hopkins very strongly. When invited to hear this author in Curzon Chapel, Evan went there with an open ear and a prepared heart. What transpired is best told in the words of his wife:

> How well I recall his coming home, deeply moved by what he had heard and experienced! He told me that he was like one looking out on a land wide and beautiful, flowing with milk and honey. It was to be possessed. It was his. As he described it all, I felt that he had received an overflowing blessing, far beyond anything that I knew. It seemed as if a gulf had come between us. We sat up late that evening talking with our Bibles before us. O, I was hungry. At last, quite simply, but very really, I too took God at His word, and accepted Christ as my Indwelling Lord and Life, and believed that He did enthrone Himself in my heart. . . .

The text that had brought such blessing was 2 Cor. 9:8, and I remember how he printed it clearly on a card, keeping it constantly before him as he feasted on the facts it revealed. Now it would be, "God is Able" that possessed his soul in new power. Then it would be, "to make all grace abound towards you;" and "All" meant all in a fuller sense than it had previously done. Next it was, "that ye always"⁻ the perpetual Present that is to be recognized⁻ "having all sufficiency"⁻ for there is no lack, no limit, no cessation of the abundant supply⁻ "in all things"⁻ heart needs, trials, disadvantageous circumstances, Christian service⁻ "might abound unto every good work!" Christ had indeed become to him the "Fountain within" springing up. It was not merely that his Lord would help him. It was that He would do all, and would live in him His own holy life⁻ the only Holy Life possible to us as we would often say.[4]

No one at that time could possibly have imagined the impact this experience of Evan Hopkins would have on the Church of Christ. He became truly inflamed with a desire to see the Lord's people "possess their possessions." So strongly did he feel the needs of struggling, oft-defeated Christians, that the boundless provision to meet those needs became the central theme of his messages. Surrender and Sanctification by Faith rang through every address, given at conferences, house meetings, and especially at conventions.

And so it was that Evan Hopkins became a Bible expositor who possessed a gift for clarifying deep truths in such a manner as to dispel confusion and prepare the way for immediate action and faith. His teaching reveals clearly that he had first received a glimpse of the natural depravity of the human heart. He was convinced also from personal experience and scriptural knowledge that all the self-efforts of a life-time would never effect a cleansing or produce real godliness.

It is important to note how the search for "deeper-life" truth followed the great ingathering of the 1859 revival. When people are genuinely born of God, they are hungry for more. This movement owed its rapid growth, therefore, to the prepared hearts ready for this truth. Thus it was that in the early 1870's, various meetings for the promoting of personal holiness were convened such as those at Broadlands, Oxford, and Brighton. These led to the first convention being held at Keswick in 1875. Mr. Hopkins was not present but, commencing the following summer, he attended without a break for thirty-one consecutive years.

It is inspiring to study how the Lord raised up stalwarts to propagate the good news of Full Salvation in Britain and America and many other parts of the world. Nor is it surprising that opposition to the teaching arose in violent force. Mr. Webb-Peploe, a comrade in the conflict for holiness, wrote to Mr. Hopkins:

> I do not know what you find among your intelligent folk, but down here, even among orthodox Evangelicals, I am looked upon as "half a black sheep." This is the trial of our faith, I suppose; for one would expect true brothers to have an understanding heart. They ask me to preach, but look half-askance and are afraid of what is taught. They cannot deny it, but dare not, it would seem, accept it with humble boldness and faith. God help us all![5]

This fellow-champion of the faith, however, proceeded to observe what soldiers of the cross have always learned, that truth will conquer and that the reproach of Christ can bring only good to those who remain identified with the most maligned One of all, Who calls us to follow in His steps. Mr. Webb-Peploe continues:

While enemies are many and strong, it is a comfort to know that there are some at least, who, like ourselves, are knit together in an inner and yet faithful friendship through the blessed and happy work of the last two years. I feel as if you and Thornton might have been my friends from youth, and I trust you as I would my oldest friends. Well, why is this, but that there is a spiritual freemasonry which the outer world cannot apprehend, but which creates fellowship at once where the secret of the Lord is known and enjoyed? Let us thank God and take courage, amid all the present necessity, and go on our way rejoicing, even if we are called to suffer shame for His Name's sake.[6]

Many have made great differences between the Keswick teaching and that of John Wesley. But let us just look at several of Mr. Wesley's statements concerning the doctrine of Christian Perfection, which prove that both he and others like Evan Hopkins were endeavoring to present to others the same message: the victorious life of the Living Christ being lived out in human persons. Wesley had met with those who rested on an experience rather than "Christ living in me, the hope of glory," and doubtless sought to rectify these false assumptions made by those who little comprehended his much misunderstood doctrine. He writes:

For, by that faith in His life, death, and intercession for us, renewed from moment to moment, we are every whit clean and there is not only now no condemnation for us, but no such desert of punishment as was before, the Lord cleansing both our hearts and lives. By the same faith we feel the power of Christ every moment resting upon us, whereby alone we are what we are, whereby we are enabled to continue in spiritual life, and without which, notwithstanding all our present holiness, we should be devils the next moment.[7]

The holiest of men still need Christ as their Prophet, as "the light of the world." For He does not give them light but from moment to moment: the instant He withdraws all is darkness. They still need Christ as their King: for God does not give them a stock of holiness. But unless they receive a supply every moment, nothing but unholiness would remain.[8]

We also quote a paragraph from D. W. Lambert who was a student under Samuel Chadwick and afterwards a lecturer at Cliff College, England.

> Evan Hopkins' emphasis in teaching Holiness is stated very clearly in his book, *The Law of Liberty in the Spiritual Life*. He prefers the figure of counteraction to that of eradication. Actually we need to remember that these are both figures of speech aimed at expressing the way God deals with sin in the human heart. The danger to our minds of the former term is that it seems to imply a necessary continuance of sin in the heart. On the other hand, we must remember that the latter term may rule out the essential thought of continuous relationship, a walking in the light, a being filled with the Spirit that is essentially a moment by moment experience. Evan Hopkins, however, in spite of the figure he uses, proclaims a continuous and full deliverance from sin for those who will fulfill the conditions. Most of all, he lived that holy life which bears witness to the fullness of the blessing he enjoyed.[9]

One could never understand the earnest passion displayed in Evan Hopkins' loving battle for sanctification and deep spiritual reality, if one overlooked the glimpse he had obtained of the sin of the natural heart. This is displayed most clearly in the first chapter of his book, *The Law of Liberty in the Spiritual Life:*

> This inheritance from Adam is an offense against God, the cause of all human miseries, and it demanded the ultimate sacrifice of the blessed Son of God. It is an entrenched, dominant principle in the center of our being. It has thrown a

chain over all our faculties. It makes the possessor a spiritual deaf-mute whose ear is closed to the clearest voice from Heaven and whose tongue is dumb, when it should be singing God's praises and proclaiming Christ's salvation.

In one of his booklets, Mr. Hopkins enumerates five ingredients of this vital experience. They are:

1. It is a condition of soul-harmony with God. You are Christians but is there no matter of controversy between your soul and God? A very little thing it may be; but you have not yielded your will about it. God has put His finger upon it, and it has given you a struggle. Perhaps you call this spiritual conflict. Is it not really spiritual rebellion?

2. It is a condition of spiritual equipment. You are an instrument. The Master wants to put His hand upon you. Are you ready? Are you fit? I see a carpenter going into his shop; he has a beautiful piece of mechanism to do, and his whole soul is fixed upon doing this work well. He takes up a chisel, but there is no edge to it, and at once, he lays it aside and takes up another. Why is the chisel not used? It is there to be used. Because it is not fit for the Master's use.

3. It is a state of preparedness for trial and suffering. You say, "I was so put out this morning; I was taken unawares." Then you were not in the blessing, evidently. You say you understand all about it and that you received it so many weeks ago, or only yesterday. That may be, but you have not been abiding in it. It has to be maintained moment by moment.

4. It means readiness for conflict. What I am privileged to see is Christ getting the victorious position for me, and I am to occupy it by faith. Then I am strong; then I am a Christ-enclosed man; my feet are firmly planted down.

5. It is a condition of spiritual intelligence. You are quick to detect the will of God. You are quick to hear the voice of God. You are ready to obey promptly, without asking questions.[10]

Rev. Hopkins and his wife carried on their pastoral work in Richmond for twenty-three years. It was while they were resident here that Mrs. Penn-Lewis removed to Richmond as her husband had been appointed Borough Accountant of the town. They soon decided that Holy Trinity Church would be their spiritual home, and so it was that the hungry-hearted Mrs. Penn-Lewis found through the preaching of Evan Hopkins what she so much desired. "Have you victory over sin?" was the poignant question put to her by Mrs. Hopkins, and she had to confess that she had not heard of such possibilities. Such are the remarkable guidings of providence when souls are led to a specific place to receive definite help on their pilgrimage. God will turn worlds upside down to get a hungering soul to a place where someone can tell them of the possibilities of grace.

Three children were born to the Hopkins. The two sons, Evan and Horace, followed their father's footsteps into the ministry and their daughter, Maude, married a vicar.

Calls to labor elsewhere came to Rev. Hopkins and his wife but they felt they were in the will of the Lord where they were. Thus Mr. Hopkins was able to carry on his ministering at conventions for the promotion of the deeper life. In 1893, however, he felt led to take over a parish of six thousand inhabitants at St. Luke's. Here he was blessed with very reliable evangelical curates, one of these for a time being his elder son, Evan. This gave him much opportunity to travel and speak and teach at "Deeper Life" conferences and conventions.

For some time, friends had advocated that he be given opportunity to travel full-time with this message, but it was not until 1906 that he had the assurance from God that it was in the divine will that he should do so. Leaving his pastorate at St. Luke's, he moved to a country house in Surrey called "Woburn Chase." Here God's servants from afar often visited him, including Dr. S. D. Gordon from America.

Besides *The Law of Liberty in the Spiritual Life* mentioned before, Evan wrote numbers of books and booklets on the subject of the Sanctification of the Believer; among them were: *Talks with Beginners in the Divine Life; The Way of Deliverance; The Holy Life,* a book for Christians seeking the rest of faith; *The Walk That Pleases God; Steps Upward; Unclaimed Privileges,* and others.

In all his works, as well as in his addresses, Evan Hopkins emphasized repeatedly that present victory is attainable here and now through a present Christ. From one message on this subject we quote:

> The present Christ is the power of an endless life. The present living Christ can know of no overcoming force. The present Christ is for ever the exalted and supremely victorious One, Who is over all things and all tendencies to evil. He has entered into the realm where the world and every earthly thing is forever under His feet. He stands triumphantly over every foe. And faith is the link between Him Who is the overcoming One and the soul that desires to enter into His life of triumph.
>
> What is faith? It is not the trying to overcome, but it is the overcoming. It needs a quiet waiting upon God, to grasp the fact that Christ has overcome⁻ a calm, believing entrance of the soul, which has forsaken the strain of self, into the repose of Christ. The effect in the sphere of experience may be immediate. We are dealing with the unseen, but we are dealing with realities. The one supreme Reality is the living Christ; let the whole soul be centered there, and then that which alone is real and potent is known and felt.[11]

His emphasis on prayer was closely intertwined with his convictions concerning the sanctified life:

> The whole question of our life depends on its being full of prayer; and the virtue of our prayer rests on three things. Not doctrines, not views, but on conditions! There is first, the

condition of peace; the Atonement has been found and accepted, and we know and are persuaded that all is right between ourselves and God. There is, next, the condition of purity; not a process of cleansing, but a fellowship with Him Who is the Separate One, so that there is an instantaneous appropriation of Christ¯ a sanctity which is not judicial but experimental. And there is, to complete and crown those two, a state of power¯ the power of the Holy Ghost, Who takes Christ and all His resources, and makes Him our own.

Let these preliminary conditions be present, and prayer is certain to be prevailing and mighty. But the peace, the purity, and the power may all be interfered with by something we tolerate in ourselves. Then what is wanted is not an earnestness and agony of a supplication, but the single eye to see what is wrong, and the decision to let it go. It means an attitude of thoroughness in settling the question of sin; and it is no good slurring that over. It may be a great fight but you cannot make progress until it is settled. Our fellowship with Christ depends on it, and fellowship is more than the safety of salvation. It is a delicate and sensitive habitude of the soul, which may, so easily and so mournfully, be spoiled and lost.

Therefore, let our action be prompt and positive. You may say, "O Lord, enable me to do this," or you may say, "Yes, Lord," and really do it; and the latter is the right course. Nor need we despair, because the demand and the sacrifice are high and searching. For then Christ enables us, giving what He commands and then commanding whatever He wills. He removes the hindrance, breaks the barriers down, and Himself leads us back into the conditions of purity, peace and of power.[12]

This faithful minister preached his last sermon in May, 1916. He used that wonderful text in Hebrews 7:25, which he liked to render, "He is able to be saving, to the very end, those who are in the habit of coming unto God through Him." His health was now much broken but he lingered on, giving continued "eventide witness" to all who came to see him.

Not long before his death, his wife had read to him Psalm 91. One morning she sang, "I Need Thee Every Hour." He feebly joined in and they altered the words of the chorus of the last stanza to:

> "I have Thee, oh, I have Thee!
> Every hour I have Thee."[13]

On the morning of March 10, 1919, Evan Hopkins passed on to be with his Lord forever. At the funeral there rang out from the lips of many the following words from Miss Havergal's hymn which he had so often joined in singing at Keswick:

> "Like a river glorious
>   Is God's perfect peace,
> Over all victorious
>   In its bright increase."[14]

Mary Mozley

She Chose The Good Part

Mary Mozley stood on board the Llandovery Castle, waving good-bye to friends and relatives. She was about to begin that long voyage which would take her to her chosen mission field. The future was mercifully veiled from the young voyager as she watched the receding shores of her native land. Little did she realize that she would be given only nine brief years to serve her Savior among the natives of the Congo before being called Home, for she was still in her twenties and life seemed to stretch out ahead. But brief though her life was to be, it would be one filled to the full with learning those lessons which would fit her for her everlasting reign with Christ. When the final call was to come, Mary Mozley would be ready!

Mary was born October 9, 1887, and passed a happy though somewhat uneventful childhood in the vicarage at South Muskham, England. When still only seven she showed an interest in the things of God but it was in her late teens, during a Bible Study being given by her mother, that she entered into New Life and yielded herself to God. She had previously attended Church Missionary Society Summer Schools during the years 1905-8, and after a prolonged talk with Dr. Jays, felt called to be a medical missionary.

Confiding to a friend, Mary told her she was quite sure of her call, but that it would entail her becoming a nurse. For months, she would turn her head away when she saw a nurse, so abhorrent were the thoughts of hospital training, yet later, when she entered Nottingham General Hospital, she was able to say, "I delight to do Thy will, O God."[1]

It was not long before Mary became known among her friends as one utterly uncompromising when it came to anything evil. When unsavory subjects were laughed about by her nursing companions, her face gave a resolute rebuke to the others, so it was not often that such conversation arose in her presence.

Four other nurses shared a room with her, and Mary did not shirk her responsibility in trying to set the tone among them. One of them, who was feeling the utter sense of loneliness after leaving home, told how she was amazed when each of the girls would open their Bibles and read verse about among themselves. In spite of her religious principles, however, Mary was not morbid, and could enjoy good, wholesome fun as much as the others.

Her thoughtfulness, too, was noticed by other nurses especially when, now and then, they would find a small gift or a good book mysteriously appearing on their bedside table, or when they would discover, unexpectedly, a welcome hot water bottle tucked into their bed on a cold winter's night.

Her term completed at Nottingham, Mary took further training at Nightingale Home, Derby, where she acted as Surgical Sister for twelve months and then took her missionary course in Ireland under the Faith Mission. She was very concerned that she be guided of God and wrote:

> I want to tell you that since coming here⁻ and before⁻ I have been praying so much for guidance as to the next step. I have been waiting for a definite call like C___. Well, I have not got it, yet the last few days it has been so much on my mind that perhaps I ought to make the next move. I feel perhaps God is wanting me to offer to the A. I. M. (Africa Inland Mission). I pray that this may be His will; it is difficult

to know sometimes the right path. But what have I given Him for all He has given me? And this birthday I wanted very specially to give myself anew to Him for service in Africa. Do pray I may have the definite assurance if this is His will for me. I feel so spiritually unfit, yet I pray that He will refine and purify and fit me, if indeed this great privilege is for me.[2]

Her call to be a missionary was not like that of others she had known, but in her agony about it she had cried out, "Lord, if it be Thou, bid me come unto Thee on the water." And He had replied, "Come."[3]

Mary naturally felt a wrench as she faced parting with all she had held dear and she realized that for those left behind, the pain of parting would be even greater. "The verse that comes into my mind," she writes, "is that one about a sword piercing through the heart. And it means that at this time. Yet for our dear ones as for ourselves, the knowledge that the sword is held in pierced Hands and the piercing is guided in the highest wisdom and the deepest love is more than comforting."[4]

But partings do not last forever. The Llandovery Castle bore the young missionary safely to Cape Town where it berthed for a short time while waiting to unload some of its cargo. Mary watched the movement of people on shore, and then noticed that there was a Red Cross ship anchored nearby. As she became aware of a Red Cross nurse in her nicely starched uniform standing beside her on the deck, she passed through a brief struggle. "Could I not also have won position and honor in this profession?" she asked herself. "Have made a name for myself? Could I not have brought joy too to the sick?"[5] It was the old form of temptation recorded in Scripture when, in the wilderness, the tempter held out to Christ a way in which He could avoid the cross and gain some honor to Himself.

But the One Who was ever present helped Mary to gain the victory. As her eyes turned back to the dockside, an

African's uplifted face spoke to her of the thousands of people who still sat in darkness and the shadow of death. "The dream of worldly advancement faded," she tells us. "How gladly and cheerfully I go forward at His call to the needy, longing, dying souls in their helplessness to 'spend and be spent' in His service as long as He shall allow me; and may He grant me to lay down my life, day by day, for Christ and for Africa, counting nothing 'dear unto myself.'"[6]

Finally her long voyage was over. Landing in Mombassa, a long trip overland lay before her. Strange sights met her eyes wherever she went, and adaptation to a new country and a new people was the next lesson that she was to learn.

On the mission station, Mary not only had to immediately confront the language barrier, but soon came to feel the encroaching darkness of heathendom. All this made her most conscious of some lack in her innermost being. She confided, in a letter home: "I write like this because it strikes me so, as a newcomer to the mission field. I realize how great and necessary a thing it is to be filled with the Holy Ghost, that one's work and life may be the expression of the 'working of His power,' working 'within me mightily.' The life of a missionary should indeed be earnest and intense. The issues seem so vital."[7]

In another letter she shows what were her priorities: "We long, as you do, I know, that Christ in His own loveliness may attract and win their lives. Only by prayer and His power is this possible."[8]

Eighteen months later, Mary had an experience which marked her religious life. She wrote to a friend:

> I seem to have no news, though there is one lovely piece of news that fills my heart with singing. You know how I have been seeking a clean heart. I think I had an intellectual conception of what it was. I have been reading Mr. Wilkes'

book on "Faith," and I knew I had not the experience. In this book Mr. Wilkes says something to the effect that "Faith is not vague, but asks for and definitely receives blessing." I knew I could not say that I had "definitely received" a clean heart, though up to a point I had trusted for one.

We decided to seek the Lord for definite heart-cleansing, for if our hearts were really cleansed we could not say, "I do not know whether I have a clean heart or not." For about a week God dealt with us, and kept us seeking. Then the Friday night before Whit Sunday the Lord graciously heard, and filled me with such a wonderful peace, the like of which I had never known before. All the darkness went, and I could only praise, for I knew the Comforter had come to dwell in my heart.[9]

As she became aware of the gross darkness around her into which no ray of the Gospel had shone, she knew she needed a love beyond a human love, and she wrote of this burden in a letter:

God has spoken much to my heart these last days from Ezek. 9:8 and the passage in Gen. 44 where Judah pleads with Joseph for Benjamin. I have been praying that the Lord would give me more love and a greater burden for these lost ones who are perishing, as indeed I still pray, for my heart seems so cold, and I seem to care really and truly so little for what it means for one soul to PERISH.

Genesis 44 seemed to speak to my heart as never before of God's love for a single soul, taking Jacob as a picture of God, and then Judah says: "How shall I go up to my father and the lad be not with me?" It makes me long to live so near to God that through me He may reach those He is longing after with such tender love.[10]

What a premium this missionary put upon not only her own prayer life, but also upon her dependence upon the prayers of others: "C. says she feels as if prayer at home were slacking off. We here, these days, are feeling the awful power of evil. Oh, we do long for more prayer; the work is just hopeless without it. If only those at home could half realize what work with a force of prayer behind it means! It is wonderful. Without it there is a dark and hopeless feeling, go forward as you may."[11]

Previous to coming out to Africa, Mary had maintained a regular prayer hour from six to seven each evening, and even though members of the family were enjoying fellowship in one another's presence, she would quietly leave their company to go to her room regardless of how cold it was, in order to spend that hour alone with God. But on the mission field in heathen Africa, after realizing the terrible need, she increased her prayer time even though the days were so busy and demands upon her time were multiplied.

When the day's work was done and night had fallen, her light would be on the last of all, and one would find her under her mosquito netting with her Bible or her good devotional book. Then, at four in the morning, she was up to get some good hours with her Bible before the day started, which always begins very early in equatorial climates. Her knowledge of God, His will, His methods, and His ways were learned in the time she took daily with the Word and in prayer. In her notes that she made while having her quiet time, there are jottings and comments on Scriptures which had been made real to her in prayer. She writes home:

> Somebody suggested this thought to me, and it came home to me the other day in reading about Christ in Gethsemane̅ that the way to show true sympathy is not to pity, but to stand by and strengthen the sufferer to do God's will. And in Gethsemane, when Christ turned to the three for sympathy, it was with the words, "watch with Me," "stand by Me." He asked for no pity, but for the strengthening which might seem a feeble help, just that they might let their presence and prayer tell there for Him, to strengthen Him to do the will of God. . . .
>
> Surely this world is no happy place to live in. If ever it seemed good, in these days God does seem to be unloosing the bands which tied us to it, and making void the charms

which once drew us. I have never realized as I do now the drawing power of God, in longing for the "new heaven and new earth wherein dwelleth righteousness." This poor old world seems rushing to its doom. Mr. Downing says that the native Christians here say they have *never* experienced the power of the evil one in the strong temptations they have to endure as now, and I, personally, can say the same. *Yet God reigneth.* Far above, all our hearts are in His keeping.[12]

Reading in Acts 1 just now the R. V. struck me. "Ye shall receive the power (dynamite) of the Holy Ghost coming upon you (A. V. m) and ye shall be my witnesses." So the conclusion forms itself that without His Spirit we are not His witnesses, though we may preach and expound the truths of God. And I like to think of that receiving of power, not as a great experience and consciousness of power, but rather that it is an experience of our utter weakness, together with a dependence, a leaning on, and an absorption into God. Power to know our helplessness, power to lean on and look to Him. Then the dynamite accomplishes the impossible for God. I long more than words can say to experience this in my own life, as I know you do in yours. Let us pray more for each other that this holy anointing may be ours.[13]

I was so struck last night by that verse in the first of Mark: "Whose shoes I am not worthy to stoop down and unloose." Not worthy even to humble myself before Him! How truly nothing we are! And yet by His grace and transforming power "made heirs of God," and chosen to be the Bride of Christ. What abounding, immeasurable grace![14]

When the Holy Spirit indwells the heart, He is jealous that the heart be wholly the Lord's and that there be a wise expenditure of that valuable commodity¯ time. How He faithfully chides one, not only for sin, but also for neglecting the wisest possible use of our talents and time. Mary showed that she was sensitive to the Spirit in this regard:

I began playing on the Hurlburts' harmonium after they had gone, and kept it up until it was too late to do anything. I felt I ought to get away somewhere alone, as up to then the day had been so busy. I wish I had. It is one of the saddest failures to miss meeting Him when He calls. "The voice of My Beloved". . . "He cometh leaping over the hills," so eager, longing for communion and found me more interested in hymn playing and turned away disappointed. I grieved much over it. There, I am telling you. You will pray much for me, won't you? It is like an S. O. S. call to you, I need it, oh so much.[15]

The following entries reveal that Mary was continually receiving further light on the value of prayer in her life and on a closer walk with her Lord:

February 3, 1919. I seem to be learning more and more since coming here, and especially lately, of the value of prayer, and more and more I long so to *know* God and *obey* Him that prayer will be *living* to me, bringing answers from Him Who said, "If ye ask . . . I will do," and coupled it all up with obedience. Since I have been on the Field, I have begun to know what it *feels* like to have people praying for me. You can *feel* it, literally, and miss it too, when it is not there. Just a kind of powerful backing; a current that lifts you and helps you along. Ah! how describe it?[16]

August 29, 1919. Sometimes I wonder how much God is delayed by us. If ever anyone needed to walk with God, we do here. If ever the devil fought against such a fellowship, he does here. If ever a life needed to pray or needed prayer it is out here. The glint and glamour that overshadows the mission field fades into gray mist out here. There is no glamour, but stern reality; overwhelming almost at times are the forces arrayed against us: the "world lieth in the evil one." Yet there is light, not the glint and glamour of heroism, but the Light that shines above us on the way, "Looking unto Jesus." "They looked unto him and were radiant" (Psa. 34:5).[17]

October 26, 1919. If we believe that "the path of the just is as a shining light which shineth more and more unto the perfect day," surely we find that the day which is called "today" is intended to be the brightest and fairest day we have ever spent.[18]

November 13, 1919. I am reading Mme. Guyon's life over again, and how she was brought through an experience of deep loneliness and later realized it was God crucifying her with Christ. How else could deep heart sorrow be borne, but for the thought that to the loving and obedient heart that present experience, whatever it be, is the will of God, and there it is we may find Him.[19]

A much needed furlough began in March, 1921, but she was back again on the field in May, 1922 and hard at it, trying to complete the translation of St. Mark's Gospel in Logo. Looking back over the years, Mary relates how the need for a translation of the New Testament had seemed paramount on their first arrival. She explains to a friend:

In 1916, when the work was first opened in this tribe, the language was unreduced and unknown to Europeans. I think no one had attempted anything beyond three typewritten sheets of words and sentences gathered by an itinerant missionary on his way through the tribe. These my sister and I pored over as a precious treasure when we first began, trying to find out the different meanings of various words in the sentence⁻ until by the help of our first bright language boy, Barangi, we found the majority wrong, and the whole unreliable. So we put them away and after trying through the Government language⁻ the lingua franca, Bangala⁻ we found inadequate, we struggled on with Barangi unaided.

That was seven years ago⁻ a long time, and we ought to know more Logo than we do, but there have been so many interruptions, through sickness, travel, and the furlough home, that the time given to actual study of it is reduced to about

four and a half years. And now we are hoping very soon to
have St. Mark's Gospel ready to send for publication to the
British and Foreign Bible Society.[20]

The difficulties had been great yet Mary could write:

> Again and again we have found the Lord's wonderful
> help in things which it was unlikely we could ever have
> discovered without it. Not the gift of tongues by any means!
> The struggle is hard and up-hill, and the more you feel you
> ought to know, the less you actually seem to know. Much
> depends on your native teacher; you are at his mercy and
> your progress seems to depend on his intelligence. At present
> we have one who is fairly good and keenly interested if we
> test out any translations with him.
>
> The other day he quietly but firmly disagreed with the
> order of events in the "House built on a rock," which I was
> laboriously trying to get into some kind of intelligible Logo.
> "And the rain descended and floods came and the wind blew."
> I read what I had got and waited expectantly to be corrected.
> He repeated it thoughtfully, then shook his head. "No‾ the
> wind blew and the rain descended and the floods came" was
> the order he preferred. Out here a big storm is ushered in by
> a huge wind, so in his mind that must come first. This just
> shows the accuracy of their minds for detail. I'm sure I had
> never noticed the order before.[21]

It was often difficult to find the exact idiom to use. Tribal
customs and culture played such a large part in the meaning of
words. At one stage, Mary had difficulty in conveying the fact
that Jesus was "set at naught." Masabe, who was now helping
them in the translation, thought and thought. "Put for nothing,"
Mary suggested as being the most sensible suggestion, but her
helper shook his head saying, "No, the Logo don't say that."
The conversation went back and forth and numerous suggestions
were made, but nothing fit the exact thought which she felt

Scripture gave. Some weeks passed and Masabe was back again with the suggestion that "to put your eyes white" was the nearest idiom for the "being set at nought."[22]

Little did Mary know during those busy days how brief this second term of service would be! But she had been learning spiritual lessons fast and developing a maturity in Christ which was surprising for one her age. A few extracts from her letters and diary reveal how the Spirit gave her understanding as to God's ways:

> Oct., 1920. How true it is that the nearer we get to Him, the more we see that it is not an "I" changed and renovated, but the old "I" crucified, which has to be "reckoned dead" continually, that He may come in His fullness. "Not even faith, but He, Himself."[23]

> Nov. 18, 1920. We are never in danger of loving too much, but too little, and truly to love means truly to suffer, for "love beareth all things" and "is not easily provoked." Now I know it behooves us not to criticize, for we cannot gauge the struggles of another soul; but it does behoove us to love and love on, and bear all things, and not be easily provoked with most provokable things and to trust in God. That is the love we want, the love we need, and the love we must have to be anything for God. We must suffer, love, pray, trust, and He will work for us.[24]

> Sept., 1921. We serve God in waiting when He so plans it more than in useless activity when He does *not* plan that. "Be still and know that I am God." God teach us so.[25]

> Oct. 6, 1922. Life is quiet here, just ourselves on the station. The work seems growing. It is plodding, up-hill work just now, sowing the seed, line upon line, line upon line, and not even "by the line," it would appear at times, but by isolated letters! God make us true and faithful.[26]

Feb. 4, 1923. More and more I learn the value of prayer and see that God does really mean what He says about answering the prayers of His people. Not, as Mr. Hurlburt says, so much for our "praying hard," as we say sometimes, but in getting near enough to God that He may hear our simple and quiet request. Not for our "much speaking," but as we are "near to Him" are we heard. And I have much to ask for you all, and for the work and for myself. God teach us how to pray in a way that will bring glory to Him, and blessing to those for whom we pray.[27]

Oct., 1923. I am seeking a deeper, fuller life in Him, really to know God and be lifted from the shallow superficiality of religious life and experience into the knowledge of the love of God. How easily we may *drift*. God help me to *lay hold* of life intensely, and live it all deeply for and with Him. How great He is, marvelous, loving.[28]

Nov. 13, 1923. I was studying Philippians a little and it seems as I read, as though the key of the epistle is the verse, "He which hath begun a good work will perfect it." How beautifully then the three prison epistles fit into each other. Colossians the Head: Ephesians, the Body, the Church; Philippians the Individual, who forms part of the Church. God's work of perfecting in the individual's heart, as Christ was perfected through suffering. "He which hath begun . . . will perfect." "God worketh in you." "I can do all things through Him." "Not already perfect, but I press on." "My God shall supply all your need." "Rejoice in the Lord always." What perfection![29]

Nov. 17, 1923. I have done nothing to write interestingly about. My life seems to be a dull routine to write of, and yet it is that which makes up life on the main. How much harder it is to be brave and happy in routine than in facing new and sensational experiences! The eternal plod of a rut needs more grace and help from God, I find, than crossing new country. I am so tempted to become grumbling in spirit and unthankful and joyless, and to lose opportunity of helping others and enlivening their ruts.[30]

Although the pathway may grow brighter for the more mature follower of the Master, the tests are more stringent and the demands of discipleship more exacting as spiritual life progresses. As the mountain climber starts out with zest on his climb to the heights he is enamored with the scenery, for as yet, his energies have not had the demands made upon them which will eventually cause fatigue and over-weariness. So it is with the Christian who is not content to dwell on the flats and the valley, but is ever attaining new altitudes of grace. Mary found this true in the goals she had set for herself:

> It comes to me how comparatively easy it used to be to walk with Him to what it is now, and I am tempted to long for the old days⁻ like Job. But somehow I think those were our "school-days"⁻ learning about Him, being taught how we should trust Him⁻ and these are the "after days" when the "school" knowledge has to be turned to practical value in order that we may take our place in life "out in the world," to step on in faith and turn to present, practical use the blessed "school-day" lessons. God grant that we fail not.[31]

During Mary's morning and evening devotions, she marked down verses which stood out to her and added her inspired thoughts upon them. Her sister who wrote her biography has included, in the last two chapters, some of these comments which came to Mary in her quiet hour:

> Matt. 3:17. God's testimony to a hidden life in humble obscurity for thirty years. "My beloved Son, in whom I am well pleased."

Matt. 23:19. God's side always exceeds and surpasses man's side. Man's consecration is completed and crowned by God's sanctification. It is God Who completes what we in our incompleteness are unable to do, try as we may. Therefore, the final move must come from God or it is imperfect.

Mark 11:17. If my heart is not a "house of prayer," it is a den of thieves.

2 Cor. 3:3. We cannot all be apostles, but we all ought to be "Epistles known and read of all men"; love letters of Jesus to the world. Written not with the "ink" of personal influence which fades with the passing of the individual.

1 John 5:14. "He heareth us." "I" am the prayer God hears. If "I" and "my petition" fail to agree, it is the voice of my life ("I") which He hears. "Time, as we look back on it from the 'land of far distances,' will seem but a little hollow scooped out on the plain of eternity for the building work to be done" (copied).[32]

Nov. 12 (Evening). "Having nothing and yet possessing all things." My hand is tiny in its grasp; God's boundless¯ infinite. Let go thine all, it is but as "nothing" and then let those Infinite Hands hold all and possess all for thee. That only which He holds for thee is thine to possess.[33]

We note from the above what familiarity Mary had gained from reading and meditating on the Word of God. She was ripe for Heaven, and God was about to pluck His ripened sheaf though the work she was doing still seemed so vital and necessary. The uphill climb was almost finished; just a little while and the hazards of traveling would be over and she would arrive HOME.

"Peace, perfect peace, by thronging duties pressed? To do the will of Jesus, this is rest" had been one of Mary's favorite hymns.[34] Now it seemed that it was the Divine will to take his weary servant home to himself. Mary had found herself becoming very tired. She had been shouldering heavy loads, for a much valued missionary doctor had recently died, leaving a lack of experienced personnel on the station. This had added to her already full program.

On the 25th of November, 1923, she took a chill and asked for an injection of quinine. The nearest doctor was some 200 miles away but, when Blackwater fever was diagnosed, he was sent for immediately and her sister notified. It was evident to all that she was failing. It would be but a brief ten days before her last lap of the journey had been wearily trudged and her work laid down.

On the 4th of December, early in the morning, her spirit joined the Lord Whom she had served and Whose friendship she had so ardently cultivated. She would not be greeting a stranger for she had often met Him and thus had come to know Him through the medium of His Word and prayer. He whose spirit beats a path of prayer daily to the Throne of Grace is not in danger of losing his way in the emergencies of life. The sustaining grace of her Lord Jesus Christ had nurtured Mary through varied circumstances, and now was at her side when she passed beyond the vale of time into the presence of the King.

> Safe home, safe home in port;
>   Rent cordage, shattered deck,
> Torn sails, provision short,
>   And only not a wreck.
> But oh! the joy upon the shore,
> To tell the voyage perils o'er.

(Permission granted for use of direct quotes from the biography of Mary Mozley by Catherine S. Miller of the Africa Inland Mission).

Bishop Asbury

THE PROPHET OF THE LONG ROAD

In the Midlands of England, in the county of Staffordshire, a child was born to a couple living near Birmingham, on August 21, 1745. The father was a gardener to two of the more affluent landowners in the district. Francis, for so they named the child, soon had a baby sister who was idolized by the family but who died very early in life. In her sorrow, the mother turned to God. More and more she read her Bible, and finally invited the much-despised Methodists into her home.

Methodism itself was to fight every inch of its way into the heart of the Staffordshire people. It was in this county that Wesley received some of his roughest handling. Later, however, Wesley recorded in his journal that among the five pottery towns of this same county, the light of revival shone most brightly. The reproach had been held in an even hand with the blessing later received.

Someone has said that Methodism really had its birth in Susannah Wesley, the mother of John and Charles. And it might also be said that Elizabeth Asbury, in giving her only son to the ministry, was the mother of American Methodism. Writing about his mother, Asbury said:

> I well remember my mother strongly urged my father to family reading and prayer; the singing of Psalms was much practiced by them both. . . . As a mother above all the women in the world would I claim her for my own, ardently affectionate; as a "mother in Israel" few of her sex have

done more by a holy walk to live and by personal labor to support the Gospel, and to wash the saints' feet. As a friend, she was generous, true, and constant.[1]

Francis Asbury, even when still a boy, hated all forms of deceit and was known for his industrious habits. Writing of his early life he said:

> I abhorred mischief and wickedness, although my mates were among the vilest of the vile for lying, swearing, fighting, and whatever else boys of their age and evil habits were like to be guilty of. From such society I very often returned home uneasy and melancholy, and although driven away by my better principles, still I would return, hoping to find happiness where I never found it. Sometimes I was much ridiculed and called *Methodist Parson* because my mother invited many people who had the appearance of religion to her house.[2]

Francis began school at an early age and was reading the Bible at age six or seven. The schoolmaster, however, was a cruel man and used to beat the boy. While this treatment made the lad turn to prayer when he would be comforted by the sense of God's presence, it also gave him an aversion to school and so he did not take kindly to his father's plans for furthering his education. Leaving school in his fourteenth year, he became a business apprentice in a nearby family. Had it not been for the schoolmaster's cruelty, Francis' life would have taken a totally different direction, and America might not have received a legacy, priceless beyond measure, in the gift of Bishop Asbury.

Through the prayers and conversation of a Methodist minister, Francis was awakened to his need of salvation before he was fourteen. He now began to pray morning and evening, and became very serious, reading Whitefield's and Cennick's sermons and every good book he could lay hands on. He was born again, and was numbered among the despised Methodists.

He and his family braved much ridicule, for, unlike many around them, they were willing to hold meetings in their own homes.

At fifteen, Francis began his preaching career on a circuit which included the neighboring counties. Having been born in the fires of persecution and reproach, he did not expect to encounter anything different in his own ministry. He writes:

> Behold me now a local preacher!⎺ the humble and willing servant of any and of every preacher that called on me by night or by day; being ready, with hasty steps, to go far and wide to do good, visiting Derbyshire, Staffordshire, Warwickshire, Worcester, and all, indeed, almost every place within my reach, for the sake of precious souls; preaching generally, three, four and five times a week and at the same time pursuing my calling. I think, when I was between twenty-one and twenty-two years of age, I gave myself up to God and His work, after acting as a local preacher near the space of five years. . . .
>
> Some time after I had obtained a clear witness of my acceptance with God, the Lord showed me, in the heat of youth and youthful blood, the evil of my heart. For a short time I enjoyed, as I thought, the pure and perfect love of God; but this happy frame did not long continue, although, at seasons, I was greatly blessed.[3]

It was around this time that the needs of the American continent were becoming known among the Methodists in Britain, and a call to offer himself for the Lord's service in America came to the young itinerant. The Conference accepted him, but he found it difficult as an only son to leave father and mother for the far-off continent. Travel was not so swift in those days, and the separation was a call for deep consecration. He had not a penny in his pocket when he arrived at Bristol from which he was to sail to the New Land but friends soon supplied his immediate needs.

A week out to sea, the young missionary wrote: "Whither am I going? To the New World. What to do: To gain honor? No, if I know my own heart. To get money? No: I am going to live to God and to bring others so to do."[4]

From the very beginning, it would seem that Asbury grasped the tremendous need of the new country. He realized that it would entail travel instead of locating in one city or town. The ministers who were representing Methodism had already shown the decided tendency to settle down, and this Asbury refused to do.

By his decision to share the hardships of pioneering with the early settlers, he was able to grasp the needs of this people, and his astute mind clearly visualized the kind of church which would suit their needs. Britain, with its glorious past history, had not many corners of her country left to pioneer. The church there had adapted itself to her needs, but these were by no means identical to the needs of this vast continent of America.

Thirteen years after Francis began his ministry in America, John Wesley appointed him, together with Dr. Coke, to supervise the Methodist Church in America. From then on, he was to become known as Bishop Asbury. "I reckon him," said Dr. Dixon in a letter written to Rev. Luke Tyerman, "the second man in Methodist history; and, in the extent of his labors, and the variety of incidents connected with them, he is not second but the first man in our community."

Although not a profound scholar, Francis Asbury became reasonably familiar with Greek and Hebrew and Latin. Ever a man of strict personal discipline, he could echo a true saying that "The soul and the body make a man, and the spirit and discipline make a Christian." As his biographer puts it: "He was ever against irregularities in ecclesiastical affairs, against laxness of faith and indefiniteness of assent."[5]

As might be expected, his insistence on discipline often

produced a negative reaction. "Many were offended at my shutting them out of the society meeting," he writes, "as they had been greatly indulged before, but this does not trouble me. While I stay, the rules must be attended to, and I cannot suffer myself to be guided by half-hearted Methodists."[6]

He was also very particular as to who was allowed into the ministry. He gives this advice to those in authority under him:

> Examine well, and with caution admit men into the ministry. It is ours to plead, protest, and oppose designing men from getting into the ministry. It is our fort, stronghold, and glory, and the superior excellency of our economy that each character must undergo a strict examination every year.
>
> Put men into office in whom you can confide. If they disappoint you let them do it but once. Of all wickedness, spiritual wickedness is the greatest, and of all deception, religious deception is the worst. Fear not for the ark; God will care for His own cause. If we have not men of great talent, we have men of good hearts. Be the willing servant of slaves; but the slave to none. Put full confidence in men that merit it; be not afraid to trust young men, they are not so likely to fail as old men; young men are willing and they are able to work.[7]

Those who knew Bishop Asbury best, always considered him to be one of the most courteous and considerate of men. Yet he was conscious that not all shared this opinion. Writing to his mother he said: "'Tis one great disadvantage to me that I am not polite enough for the people. They deem me fit for the country, but not for the cities; and it is my greater misfortune I cannot, or will not learn, and they cannot teach me."[8]

Numbers never allured him; simple things held an attraction for him. Then, too, he possessed a remarkable gift of discernment, to which his biographers attribute much of his success. Henry Boehm, one of his traveling companions, wrote in his *Reminiscences* of the Bishop that "he would sit in

Conference and look from under his dark and heavy eyebrows, reading countenances and studying the character and constitution of the preachers, not only for the sake of the Church but for their own sakes. He would say to me: 'Henry, Brother A. or B. has been too long on the rice plantations or on the Peninsula. He looks pale; health begins to decline; he must go to the high lands.'"[9]

"His eyes were of a bluish cast," Boehm adds, "and so keen that it seemed as if he could look right through a person."[10]

What made this man so effective? He spent long hours in converse with One in Whose presence he took on likeness. "He was a true Methodist in prayer," his biographer Benjamin Gregory comments. "At one time it was his practice to set aside three hours of every morning for private prayer. Then he determined to pray definitely seven times a day; and afterwards he prayed for a part of every waking hour. And even when the number of preachers had grown into hundreds, he prayed separately for each one by name."

Freeborn Garrettson said of Bishop Asbury that he prayed the most and prayed the best of any man he knew. If ever a man sought to live a life of prayer it was he. "I desire that prayer should mix with every thought," Asbury writes, "with every wish, with every word, and with every action, that all might ascend as a holy, acceptable sacrifice to God.

"Arose before three. I am much employed, but it is good to make the best of every moment and carefully to fill up the space of time that may be lost. O how precious is time! Our moments though little are golden sands."

Bishop Asbury, however, was not only a man of prayer. He was also what Mr. Wesley exhorted his preachers to be ̄ a man of one Book. His references to the Bible may be found on almost every page of his Journal as the following extracts illustrate:

I spent much of my time in reading the Bible and the Greek Testament. My meditations in the Hebrew Bible have afforded me great pleasure. This is the Book I study for improvement.

My soul is stayed on the Lord, and I find great sweetness in reading the Bible, and comparing spiritual things with spiritual. Other books have too great a tendency to draw us from this the best of books. I therefore intend to read more in this and less in all others. I have found lately more sweetness and delight than ever before in reading the Old Testament. . . .

Arose as I commonly do, before five o'clock in the morning to study the Bible. I find none like it and find it of more consequence to a preacher to know his Bible than all the languages or books in the world.

Filled my minute book, and read freely in the Bible. This Book is so much hated by some. As for me, I will read it more than ever.

This morning I ended the reading my Bible through in about four months. It is hard work for me to find time for this, but all I read I owe to early rising. If I were not always to rise by five, and sometimes at four o'clock, I should have only time to eat my breakfast, pray in the family, and get ready for my journey, as I must travel every day.[11]

The Bishop did not confine his reading to the Bible, however, and was an ardent lover of Wesley's Sermons and Journals. He writes:

I have endeavored to improve my time to the best advantage in reading and have seen so much beauty and holiness that I have thirsted and long for more.

I have filled my intervals in reading my Bible, and the second volume of Mr. Wesley's sermons. O how I wish our preachers and people read his Journals, sermons and notes! Have read in the intervals of these two days twelve of Mr. Wesley's sermons. . . . The reading of Mr. Wesley's Journal has been made a particular blessing to my soul. . . . There is a certain spirituality in his works which I cannot find in any other human composition.

Bishop Asbury was also a fine singer, and "was interested, therefore, in the publication of a hymn book for the use of American Methodists."[12]

Another characteristic of this great man was his thirst for holiness as his biographer tells us:

> How passionate were his longings for holiness: "How I long to be as a pure, seraphic flame. How greatly do I desire to die to everything which does not lead me to God." Cowper's hymn was often upon his lips:
>
> "The dearest idol I have known
>   Whate'er that idol be,
> Help me to tear it from Thy throne
>   And worship only Thee.
>
> "So shall my walk be close with God,
>   Calm and serene my frame;
> So purer light shall mark the road
>   That leads me to the Lamb."
>
> . . . In my judgment no man ever lived who more steadfastly yearned after holiness than Francis Asbury. Early and late, in log cabins and beneath the star-flecked sky, in the saddle, and when standing sentry on a dangerous frontier, everywhere and always, he hungered for holiness. It was one of the two great passions of his soul‾ personal holiness‾ the other, and greater even, being the salvation and sanctification of other precious souls.[13]

"I am divinely impressed with a charge to preach sanctification in every sermon!" he writes in his journal. "I have endeavored to preach holiness faithfully, but if I had my life to live over again, I would preach it still more persistently."[14]

Bishop Asbury also felt an immense debt to the One Who was so precious to him. "If I had a thousand hearts and tongues and a million of years to live," he tells us, "all would be insufficient for paying this mighty debt of praise."[15]

Francis Asbury always lived with an acute consciousness that this earth was not his home and that material things mattered little to a Heaven-bound traveler. On June 6, 1813, he entered in his journal:

> Knowing the uncertainty of the tenure of life, I have made my will, appointing Bishop McKendree, Daniel Hitt, and Henry Boehm my executors. If I do not in the meantime spend it, I shall leave, when I die, an estate of two thousand dollars, I believe. I give it all to the Book Concern. This money, and somewhat more, I have inherited from departed Methodist friends, in the State of Maryland, who died childless; besides some legacies which I have never taken. Let it all return, and continue to aid the cause of piety.[16]

His deep sense of call and of indebtedness to Christ impelled Asbury to continue travel and public ministry right to the end. The Conference had given him a young companion whose love smoothed the rugged path toward the close of his earthly ministry.

We are indebted to his biographer, Rev. F. W. Briggs, for recording those last momentous days of Bishop Asbury:

> "Oh, let me do good whilst I may! Time is short. How my friends waste away! Yet I live. Let me live every moment to God." Thus he wrote at Charleston, when entering upon the year 1814. His physical infirmities had partly increased, and his attacks of inflammatory rheumatism and "pleuritic fever" were more and more frequent and threatening; yet he

felt as eager as ever to prosecute his immense Episcopal tours. "Arrived at Georgetown, Maryland," he writes. "I suppose I have crossed the Allegheny mountains sixty times."[17]

Continuing his travels, he became very ill and was detained at Perry Hall for three days. But he proceeded to Philadelphia where he "not only presided over the Conference, but preached with extraordinary power to crowded congregations." Hence he proceeded as far as New Jersey, when violent fever seized him, and he was laid aside for twelve weeks. From this attack he never completely rallied. He says with reference to it:

> I would not be loved to death, and so came down from my sick-room, and took to the road, weak enough. Attentions constant, and kindness unceasing, have pursued me to this place, and my strength increased daily. I look upon a martyr's life of toil, privation, and pain; and I am ready for a martyr's death. The purity of my intentions; my diligence in the labors to which God has been pleased to call me; the unknown sufferings I have endured⁻ what are these? The merit, atonement and righteousness of Christ alone, make my plea. . . . I groan one minute with pain, and shout "Glory" the next.[18]

And so he continued his travels right to the end. The last two Sabbaths, the seventy-one-year-old veteran ministered to others although the effort seemed too much for his wasted frame. Rev. Briggs describes the last hours of this untiring warrior, including the words of the Bishop's traveling companion, Mr. Bond:

> "Our dear father appears much worse. He has had a very restless night, and is, I think, in more apparent danger of approaching dissolution than I ever saw him, even in his attack in the State of New Jersey. He says himself that he is apprehensive the scene will soon close."

At eleven in the forenoon he requested that the family might be called into his room for worship. Mr. Bond then read the twenty-first chapter of the Book of Revelation, sang a hymn, and offered prayer. During these exercises he appeared to be abstracted in thought, as if by the aid of the imagery used in the chapter read, to describe the heavenly Jerusalem, he had already passed to the intended reality. He then looked at his young friend with a smile of unearthly benignity, as if to dispel the expression of distress which his countenance betrayed.

In an hour or two, Mr. Bond inquired affectionately if Christ continued to be precious, and without power to enunciate a syllable, he simply raised his hands. And then, reclining his head upon his beloved companion's arm, he calmly entered into rest. "Our dear father," wrote Mr. Bond, "has left us, and has gone to the Church triumphant. He died as he lived⁻ full of confidence, full of love⁻ at four o'clock this afternoon," (Sunday March 31, 1816).[19]

Much more could be said about such an extraordinary servant of the Lord but we close with the words of Henry Boehm, who knew him intimately, having traveled more than forty thousand miles with him: "Bishop Asbury possessed more deadness to the world, more of a self-sacrificing spirit, more of the spirit of prayer, of Christian enterprise, of labor, and of benevolence, than any other man I ever knew; he was the most unselfish being I was ever acquainted with. Beyond any other person he embodied the genius and spirit of early Methodism."[20]

NOTES TO SOURCES

Marquis De Renty

1. M. L. Christlieb, *They Found God,* (London: Unwin Brothers Ltd., 1937) pp. 32-33
2. Ibid., pp. 41-42
3. Ibid., pp. 42-43
4. Ibid., p. 43

Stephen Grellet

1. Benjamin Seebohm, *Memoirs of the Life and Gospel Labours of Stephen Grellet, Vol. I,* (London: A.W. Bennett, 1861) p. 6
2. Ibid.
3. Ibid.
4. Ibid., pp. 15-17
5. Ibid., p. 24
6. Ibid.
7. Ibid., p. 32
8. Ibid., p. 38
9. Ibid., pp. 39-40
10. Ibid., p. 342
11. Benjamin Seebohm, *Memoirs of the Life and Gospel Labours of Stephen Grellet, Vol. II,* (London: A.W. Bennett, 1861) p. 54
12. Ibid., p. 59
13. Ibid., pp. 61-62
14. Ibid., pp. 56-57
15. Ibid., p. 59
16. Ibid., p. 70
17. Benjamin Seebohm, *Vol. I,* p. 223
18. Ibid., p. 189
19. Ibid., pp. 222-223
20. Ibid., p. 226
21. Ibid., p. 301
22. Ibid., p. 281
23. Benjamin Seebohm, *Vol. II,* p. 385
24. *The American Friend,* Nov. 28, 1895

John Smith

1. Richard Treffy Jr., *Memoirs of the Life, Character, and Labours of the Rev. John Smith,* (London: William Nichols, 1867) p. 16
2. Ibid.
3. Ibid., p. 20
4. Ibid., p. 27
5. Ibid., pp. 27-28
6. Ibid., p. 36
7. Ibid., p. 121
8. Ibid., p. 170
9. Ibid., pp. 64-65
10. Ibid., pp. 134-135
11. Ibid., pp. 143-144
12. Ibid., p. 144
13. Ibid., p. 145
14. Ibid., pp. 148-150
15. Ibid., p. 215
16. Ibid., p. 220

Uncle John Vassar

1. Thomas E. Vassar, *Uncle John Vassar,* (Terra Haute: Ambassadors for Christ, Inc., 1984) pp. 51-52
2. H. A. Seyguern, "Uncle John Vassar," (*The Christian Age*, Oct. 8, 1879) p. 232
3. Thomas E. Vassar, pp. 120-122
4. Ibid., pp. 78-79
5. Ibid., pp. 65-67
6. Ibid., p. 67
7. A. J. Gordon, "Introduction," in *Uncle John Vassar,* pp. 18-33
8. Ibid., p. 30
9. Ibid., p. 182
10. Ibid.

George Railton

1. Eileen Douglas and Mildred Duff, *Commissioner Railton*, (London: The Salvationist Publishing and Supplies Ltd.) p. 35
2. Ibid., pp. 93-94
3. Ibid., pp. 92-93
4. Bernard Watson, *Soldier Saint,* (London: Hodder and Stoughton, 1970) p. 71
5. Ibid.
6. Eileen Douglas and Mildred Duff, p. 84
7. Bernard Watson, p. 69
8. Eileen Douglas and Mildred Duff, p. 100
9. Bernard Watson, p. 237
10. Ibid., pp. 238-239
11. Eileen Douglas and Mildred Duff, p. 243
12. Ibid., pp. 247-248
13. Ibid., p. 85

John G. Govan

1. J. G. Govan, *In the Train of His Triumph,* (Edinburgh: "Bright Words" Office) pp. 7-8
2. Ibid., p. 9
3. Ibid., p. 10
4. Ibid., pp. 11-12
5. Ibid., pp. 15-16
6. I. R. Govan, *Spirit of Revival,* (London: Purnell and Sons, Ltd., 1938) p. 24
7. Ibid., p. 26
8. Ibid., pp. 26-27
9. J. G. Govan, p. 27
10. I. R. Govan, p. 64
11. Ibid., p. 58
12. Ibid., pp. 62-63
13. Ibid., p. 86
14. Ibid., p. 113
15. Ibid., p. 88
16. Ibid., p. 83

Oswald Chambers

1. Gertrude Chambers, *Oswald Chambers, His Life and Work,* (London: Simpkin Marshall, 1947) p. 166

2. Ibid., pp. 52-53

3. Ibid., p. 22

4. Ibid., p. 43

5. Ibid., pp. 77-80

6. Ibid., pp. 166-167

7. Oswald Chambers, *Not Knowing Whither,* (London: Simpkin Marshall, 1946) p. 54

8. Gertrude Chambers, p. 213

9. Ibid., p. 47

10. Ibid., p. 279

11. Ibid., p. 278

12. Ibid., p. 95

13. Ibid.

14. Ibid., p.2 94

15. Ibid., p. 104

16. Ibid., p. 14

17. Ibid., p. 162

18. Ibid., p. 15

19. Ibid., p. 210

Evan Hopkins

1. Alexander Smellie, *Evan Henry Hopkins, A Memoir,* (London: Marshall Brothers) p. 22

2. Ibid., p. 25

3. Ibid., pp. 25-28

4. Ibid., pp. 54-55

5. Ibid., p. 81

6. Ibid., p. 83

7. John Wesley, *Repentance of Believers,* p. 39.

8. John Wesley, *Christian Perfection,* p. 87.

9. D. W. Lambert, *Heralds of Holiness*, (Hampton, TN: Harvey Christian Publishers Inc., 1988) p. 41
10. Alexander Smellie, p. 88
11. Ibid., pp. 204-205
12. Ibid., pp. 214-215
13. Ibid., p. 219
14. Ibid., p. 223

Mary Mozley

1. Catherine S. Miller, *The Obedience of Faith*, (London: Africa Inland Mission, 1949) p. 13
2. Ibid., p. 16
3. Ibid.
4. Ibid., p. 17
5. Ibid., p. 22
6. Ibid., p. 23
7. Ibid., p. 27
8. Ibid., p. 37
9. Ibid., p. 49
10. Ibid., p. 51
11. Ibid., p. 64
12. Ibid., pp. 67-68
13. Ibid., pp. 70-71
14. Ibid., pp. 74-75
15. Ibid., p. 76
16. Ibid., p. 77
17. Ibid., p. 89
18. Ibid., p. 92
19. Ibid., pp. 95-96
20. Ibid., pp. 126-127
21. Ibid., pp. 94-95
22. Ibid., pp. 127-128
23. Ibid., pp. 100-101

24. Ibid., p. 102
25. Ibid., p. 111
26. Ibid., p. 116
27. Ibid., p. 119
28. Ibid., p. 130
29. Ibid., p. 132
30. Ibid.
31. Ibid., p. 134
32. Ibid., pp. 140-145
33. Ibid., p. 159
34. Ibid., p. 134

Bishop Asbury

1. Ezra Squier Tipple, *The Prophet of the Long Road*, (New York: The Methodist Book Concern) p. 55
2. Ibid., pp. 40-41
3. Ibid., p. 43
4. Francis Asbury, *Journal*
5. Ezra Squier Tipple, p. 243
6. Ibid., p. 244
7. Ibid., p. 228
8. Ibid., p. 316
9. Ibid., p. 267
10. Ibid., p. 302
11. Ibid., pp. 102-103
12. Ibid., p. 105
13. Ibid., p. 309
14. Journal, p. 427
15. Ez ra Squier Tipple, p. 310
16. Ibid., p. 284
17. F. W. Briggs, *Bishop Asbury*, p. 377
18. Ibid., p. 378
19. Ibid., pp. 388-389
20. Ezra Squier Tipple, p. 14

They Knew Their God

VOLUME ONE

Nicholas of Basle (1308-1398) : *The Friend Of God*
John Tauler (1290-1361) : *The Enlightened Doctor*
Christmas Evans (1766-1838) : *One-eyed Preacher Of Wales*
William Bramwell (1754-1818) : *Apostle Of Prayer*
Mother Cobb (1793-?) : *Saint In Calico*
Felix Neff (1798-1827) : *The Brainerd Of The High Alps*
Robert Cleaver Chapman (1803-1902) : *The Rich, Poor Man*
Holy Ann (1810-1904) : *The Irish Saint*
Isaac Marsden (1807-1882) : *Earnest Merchant Preacher*
Alfred Cookman (1828-1871) : *Washed In The Blood Of The Lamb*
Elizabeth Baxter (1837-1926) : *Christian "Heraldess"*
Lilias Trotter (1853-1928) : *The Frail Pioneer*
John Hyde (1865-1911) : *The Praying Missionary*
Samuel Logan Brengle (1860-1936) : *Soldier And Servant*
Eva Von Winkler (1866-1932) : *Mother Eva Of Friedenshort*
Samuel Morris (1872-1893) : *Angel In Ebony*
Iva Vennard (1871-1945) : *Dedicated Educator*
Johanna Veenstra (1894-1932) : *A Flame For God*

They Knew Their God

VOLUME TWO

Gerhard Tersteegeny (1697-1769) : *Recluse in Demand*
John Woolman (1720-1772) : *Friend of the Oppressed*
Elijah Hedding (1780-1852) : *The Pioneer Bishop*
Robert Aitken (1800-1873) : *Prophet of Pendeen*
Mrs. Phoebe Palmer (1807-1872) : *The Gift on God's Altar*
Robert Murray McCheyne (1813-1843) *Youthful Saint of Dundee*
William Burns (1815-1858) *The Man with the Book*
Frances R. Havergal (1837-1879) *God's Songster*
Pastor Hsi (1837-1896) *Conqueror of Demons*
George D. Watson (1845-1923) *Apostle to the Sanctified*
Jessie Penn-Lewis (1861-1927) *Overcomer*
The Three Garratt Sisters (Helena **1869-1946**) *The Three-fold Cord*
Paget Wilkes (1871-1934) *Able Defender of the Faith*
Basil Malof (1883-1957) *Apostle to Russia*
Thomas R. Kelly (1893-1941) *Searcher and Finder*
John & Betty Stam (John **1907-1934**) *Their Death was Gain*
George Henry Lang (1874-1958) *God's Obedient Servant*

They Knew Their God

VOLUME FOUR

Phillip Henry (1631-1696) and

Matthew (1662-1714) Henry : *The Making of a Commentator*

Freeborn Garrettson (1752-1827) : *Saint in the Saddle*

Catherine Garrettson (1752-1849) : *The Gracious Hostess*

John Gossner (1773-1855) : *Intrepid Adventurer in Faith and Prayer*

John Hunt (1812-1848) : *Apostle to Fiji*

Elizabeth Prentiss (1818-1878) : *The Suffering Succorer*

Lord Radstock (1833-1913) : *The Lord Who Served*

Dr. Frederick Baedeker (1823-?) : *A Man Sent from God*

Frank Crossley (1839-1897) : *God's Paymaster*

They Knew Their God

VOLUME FIVE

George Herbert (1593-1632) : *Poet of the Heavenly Court*

Miguel Molinos (1627-1696) : *The Priest Who Knew God*

Joseph Alleine (1634-1668) : *A Living Sacrifice at Thirty-four*

John Fletcher (1729-1785) : *Apostle of Madeley*

Mary Fletcher (1739-1815) : *Shepherdess of Orphans*

Frederick Oberlin (1740-1826) : *Benefactor to the Vosges Dwellers*

Samuel Pollard (1826-1877) : *He Waited for the Fulfilment of His Vision*

George Matheson (1842-1906) : *The Blind Poet Who Saw Too Much*

Jonathan Goforth (1859-1936) : *He Suffered the Loss of All Things*

Rosalind Goforth (1864-?) : *She Climbed the Ascents With God*

Kate Lee (1872-1920) : *The Angel Adjutant*

W. Graham Scroggie (1877-1954?) : *The Unusual Keswick Speaker*

They Knew Their God

VOLUME SIX

John Chrysostom (344-407) : *The Fearless Bishop*

John Brown (1722-1787) : *The Cowherd Who Became Commentator*

Charles Simeon (mid 1700's-1836) : *A Man in Touch With God*

Henry Martyn (1781-1812) : *Too Young to Die?*

Helen Ewan (early 1900's) : *A Fragrant Life*

Edward Payson (1783-1827) : *He Discovered the Secret of Being Nothing*

James Turner (1818-1862) : *God's Fisherman*

Thomas Waring (?) : *The Silent Years*

Anthony Norris Groves (1795-1853) : *Pioneer in Apostolic Principles*

Mary Bethia Groves (early 1800's) : *The Once Reluctant Missionary*

William Wilberforce (1759-1837) : *A Rich Politician Called To Be God's Prophet*

John Pierpont (early to mid 1800's) : *God Compensates His Fearless Prophet*

Johann Christoph Blumhardt (1805-1889) : *German Pastor Who Defied Devils*

E. M. Bounds (1835-1913) : *He Prayed While Others Slept*

For more information visit our website at www.harveycp.com or write to one of the addresses below.

United States

Harvey Christian Publishers Inc.
3107 Hwy 321
Hampton, TN 37658
Tel/Fax (423) 768-2297
E-mail: books@harveycp.com
Internet: www.harveycp.com

Great Britain

Harvey Christian Publishers UK
PO Box 510, Cheadle
Stoke-on-Trent, ST10 2NQ
England, U.K.
Tel. (01538) 752291
E-mail: jjcook@mac.com

OTHER BOOKS BY HARVEY

Amazing Book, The, Vol. 1
Amazing Book, The, Vol. 2
Asking Father
Call Back 1: Illness
Call Back 2: Loneliness
Call Back 3: Frustration
Call Back 4: Opposition 1
Call Back 5: Opposition 2
Call Back 6: Handicaps 1
Call Back 7: Handicaps 2
Call Back 8: Old Age
Christian's Daily Challenge, The
Covetousness
Father Calling
Him or It?
Household Foes
How They Prayed 1: Household Prayers
How They Prayed 2: Ministers' Prayers
How They Prayed 3: Missionaries and Revival
King's Diamond, The
Kneeling We Triumph 1
Kneeling We Triumph 2
Let My People Go!
New Creation, The
Royal Counsel
Royal Exchange
Royal Insignia
Royal Pilgrimage
Royal Purposes
Soul Sculpture
They Knew Their God 1
They Knew Their God 2
They Knew Their God 3
They Knew Their God 4
They Knew Their God 5
They Knew Their God 6
To Judge or Not to Judge

For more information go to: www.harveycp.com

Biographies / Autobiographies

Count Zinzendorf *by Felix Bovet*
A very well written account of an unusual man of God. Zinzendorf, a contemporary of John Wesley, founded a religious community among Moravian immigrants called Herrnhut. He also wrote hymns and various books and instituted foreign missions. 96 pages

Amanda Smith *Autobiography*
An inspiring story of a slave who relates her deliverance from bondage and her second escape from sin's bondage. Although a humble washerwoman, she was remarkably used as God's instrument to tell the story of the sanctified life to high and low. 159 pages

William Carvoss *Autobiography and Letters*
This biography illustrates how useful an ordinary lay person can become in the purposes of God. Having no special talents or even a call to preach, Carvosso was yet a "burning and shining light," and multitudes were blessed through his life and labors. His was a career from which we can all learn. 196 pages

Gerhard Tersteegen *Volume 1*
Recluse in Demand (Life and Letters)
After a very real encounter with God, Tersteegen sought a quiet life of seclusion and contemplation. However, hungry souls besieged his dwelling place, anxious to feast their souls on the Bread of Life. This book gives his story, along with a number of letters. 142 pages

CPSIA information can be obtained
at www.ICGtesting.com
Printed in the USA
FSHW04n0916150418
46978FS